PRO MOTOCROSS & OFF-ROAD MOTORCYCLE RIDING TECHNIQUES

PRO MOTOCROSS & OFF-ROAD MOTORCYCLE RIDING TECHNIQUES

DONNIE BALES
WITH GARY SEMICS

MBI Publishing Company

Dedication

This book is dedicated to the memory of Danny Hamel, Wayne Cornelius, Jeff Barbacovi, and Mark Gleckl—four enthusiasts who lost their lives during 1995. You will be forever missed.

First published in 2000 by MBI Publishing Company, 729 Prospect Avenue, PO Box 1, Osceola, WI 54020-0001 USA

© Donnie Bales, 2000

MBI Publishing Company books are also available at discounts in bulk quantity for industrial or sales-promotional use. For details write to Special Sales Manager at Motorbooks International Wholesalers & Distributors, 729 Prospect Avenue, PO Box 1, Osceola, WI 54020-0001 USA.

Edited by Sara Perfetti
Designed by Tom Heffron
Layout by Bruce Leckie

Printed in China

Library of Congress Cataloging-in-Publication Data
Bales, Donnie.
  Pro motocross and off-road riding techniques / Donnie Bales.–New ed.
    p. cm.
  Includes Index
  ISBN 0-7603-0831-4 (pbk. : alk. paper)
   1. Motocross. 2. Motorcycling. I. Title: At head of title: CyclePro.
  II. Title: Motocross and off-road riding techniques. III. Title

GV1060.12 .B35 2000
796.7'56–dc21   99-087809

On the front cover: Hailed as the most natural rider to grace the sport of motocross: Jeremy McGrath.

On the back cover: Fallen trees can be very intimidating, especially the large ones. Things such as ground clearance, traction, and gravity sometimes make it seem impossible to get over such as obstacle, period—let alone in total control. Starts can be intimidating, too. Many riders will tell you that the start is the single most important aspect of any race.

WARNING: Off-road motorcycle riding is an extremely dangerous and sometimes fatal sport. The riders depicted in this book are all professionals and are using proper protective gear under controlled conditions. Attempting to duplicate their actions may be hazardous. Readers are cautioned that individual abilities, motorcycles, race tracks, terrain, weather, and riding conditions differ, and due to these unlimited factors beyond the control of the authors, photographers, and riders quoted in this book, liability is expressly disclaimed. Do not attempt any maneuvers, stunts, or techniques that are beyond your capabilities.

Contents

Foreword

by Greg Albertyn

When I started riding motorcycles in South Africa as a child, I couldn't believe how much fun it was right from the beginning. The overall sensation and freedom it provided was incredible from day one. Soon it became an obsession and I decided to dedicate myself to the sport. Every day I wanted to learn something new, whether it was to climb a virgin hill, create a new double jump, or figure out ways to speed through corners quicker.

The funny thing is, I haven't grown out of it. Motorcycling wasn't a passing phase of childhood; instead it has been the foundation for my life. It's provided me with a sense of

relaxation, a constant source of enjoyment, and the ability to test myself both physically and mentally. I loved it so much that I started racing because I craved the competition element. To my surprise, my interest grew even greater, and I simply couldn't get enough seat time. Racing was a complete adrenaline rush that took the experience to a new level.

Fortunately I have been blessed to have won three World Championships and the 1999 AMA 250cc National title, but you don't have to race to enjoy off-road riding. Heck, you don't even have to be all that good, really! Some of my most memorable experiences have been riding with friends and traveling to new locations just to explore. Hawaii on a dirt bike, yeah, that's pretty cool.

Improving your skills is what keeps riding fresh. To me, the level of enjoyment is amplified when I am able to improve my techniques. This doesn't mean that I have to go out there and jump the biggest triple or go down the steepest hill, but the overall experience is more enjoyable as I learn new skills. Some riders will naturally get faster much quicker than others, and improvements will most definitely take time. But I always encourage people to go out there and try to challenge themselves. Always make the most of it and share the experience with others. I cannot ever see a point in my life where I would want to stop riding—it's that much fun for me. But more important than anything else, ride safe and God bless.

Born in South Africa, Greg Albertyn first claimed fame on the European Grand Prix circuit. He came to the United States in 1995, but it took him a while to adapt to the hybrid Supercross-style courses. His breakthrough came in 1999 when he won the AMA 250cc National Championship in one of the sport's best title fights.

Acknowledgments

This book would not have been published without the assistance of a lot of friends. First off, I need to thank *Dirt Rider* magazine's Ken Faught, who hooked me up with MBI Publishing Company and has been supportive and helpful throughout this project. I couldn't have done it without you, buddy. I would also like to thank Joe Bonnello and Garth Milan for their photographic assistance and Lee Klancher from MBI Publishing Company for providing me with a lot of the insight during the production of my first book. This book took more than a year to produce, and it's entirely too much for just one person to conquer by himself.

I also extend a special thanks to the professional riders who lent their time and expertise to the production of the book: Greg Albertyn, Fred Bramblett, Danny Carlson, Ricky Carmichael, Guy Cooper, Mike Craig, Ty Davis, John Dowd, Danny Hamel, Scot Harden, Steve Hatch, Doug Henry, Mike Kiedrowski, Steve Lamson, Ron Lechien, Jeremy McGrath, Scott Plessinger, Rick Sowma, Scott Summers, and Larry Roeseler. I would also like to thank Pat Schutte at PACE, the entire McGrath family, and everyone who has been supportive of this great sport.

Jeremy McGrath pioneered many of today's riding techniques while chasing six Supercross titles. He is considered the master of our sport, and his supremacy may never be equaled.

Introduction

Off-road motorcycle riding is an incredible sport that blends mechanical genius with athletic ability, finesse, and patience. It offers a multitude of challenges for riders of all skill levels and rewards us with the opportunity to interact with Mother Nature. Most important, it is perhaps the most entertaining way you can spend your time. Off-road riding is fun, and that's why most of us do it.

The intention of this book is to help you improve your riding by applying the techniques of the world's faster riders as well as those developed by motocross instructor Gary Semics, an ex-champion racer who has served as Jeremy McGrath's personal trainer.

Riders like Jeremy McGrath, Ricky Carmichael, Doug Henry, Ty Davis, Guy Cooper, Steve Lamson, John Dowd, Larry Ward, and Greg Albertyn are just a few of the top professional riders who have lent their time and expertise to this book. Inside, you'll see these riders executing the techniques that brought them success, and read their personal tips on riding.

The book is geared toward all types of off-road riding. It explores the high-flying world of Supercross and the fast-paced action of outdoor motocross, plus cross-country and enduro racing, where survival is of paramount importance.

Improving your riding technique begins with getting comfortable, and it requires that you and the bike work together as a unit. The opening chapters deal with simply making you as natural and comfortable as possible; they range from guides on riding gear to tailoring the bike to your body and riding style. The gear guide includes some tips on dealing with conditions, advice that will keep you riding through all that our friend Mother Nature can throw at you.

Perhaps the most important part of the book is the chapter on body positioning. Body position is the key to riding well and is the single most common mistake in off-road riding. If you get out of position, you will struggle to find ways to correct yourself. If you stay out of position, you will spend all of your time fighting the bike and, inevitably, fall behind. If your body is in the right place, the rest of the techniques will follow more easily. Good body position makes riding more natural and enjoyable.

The ensuing chapters take apart the basics of braking, accelerating, cornering, whoops, and jumping. These skills are a critical part of any ride, and you'll find the basics of each technique, the inside scoop from the pros, and some advanced techniques from motocross instructor Gary Semics.

What you'll discover is a basic system that you can apply to different conditions. You also see that your riding skills will improve if you learn to use blend techniques. The brakes can be used to hold a line in a corner, for example, and the throttle is a key part to how far and high you jump.

Once you learn this basic system, you can apply it to any kind of riding. There are literally millions of different situations that you can get yourself into while riding, and every possible situation can't be covered in one book, or even in a three-volume set. Applying the basic techniques to new obstacles and situations—and the fact that those obstacles are never exactly the same—is what makes off-road riding so challenging and enjoyable.

The off-road section of the book deals with conquering the most common obstacles found on the trail or the enduro circuit. Top professionals like Guy Cooper and Ty Davis give you the inside track on scaling vertical uphills, fording streams, navigating brutal ruts, banging your bars through the trees, and more.

Though this book should make you a smarter rider as you develop your skills, never forget your ultimate goal is to have a good time. For a few elite riders, off-road racing is a career. When they go to the track, their paycheck depends on where they finish. For the rest of us mortals, the difference between finishing up front or in the back of the pack is a hunk of chromed plastic and bragging rights. Find your own victories and enjoy yourself. You'll probably come home happier, and you might find that the only way to get to that next level is to relax and have fun.

The Professional Riders in This Book

A number of top-ranked professional riders lent their time and expertise to the production of this book. Not only do these guys make up the heart of this book, they are also the soul of the sport. They are the definition of fast, and have dedicated their lives to stretching that definition to new limits.

Here's a list of the riders who helped out with the book:

Greg Albertyn
Corona, California
1992 & 1993 125cc World Champion
1994 250cc World Champion
1999 AMA 250cc National Champion

Born in South Africa, Greg Albertyn first claimed fame on the European Grand Prix circuit. He came to the United States in 1995, but it took him a while to adapt to the hybrid Supercross-style courses. His breakthrough came in 1999 when he won the AMA 250cc National Championship in one of the sport's best title fights.

Danny Carlson
Sun City, California
1995 Kawasaki Race of Champions, Runner-up
1996 NMA Grand National 125cc Stock
    Intermediate Champion
1996 NMA Grand National 250cc Modified
    Intermediate Champion

Danny Carlson was one of the hottest mini riders in the mid-1990s and was so talented that Honda hired the teenager to help develop the first-ever CR80 Expert.

Ricky Carmichael
Tarpon Springs, Florida
1997–1999 AMA 125cc National
    Motocross Champion
1998 AMA 125cc Eastern Region
    Supercross Champion

Ricky Carmichael is the most dominant 125cc outdoor rider in history. Many feel that he has the potential to be considered the world's fastest racer sometime in the future. He's also well-versed in Supercross, and is currently one of the best entertainers, thanks to his incredible jumping style.

Guy Cooper
Stillwater, Oklahoma
Ex-pro motocross rider; now races off-road
1990 AMA 125cc National Champion
1994 & 1996 ISDE Gold Medalist

A natural showman, Guy won fans across the globe with aerial antics and a hard-charging style that made him a legend in motocross and Supercross. He has taken his high-flying techniques to enduro, hare scrambles, and cross-country racing.

Mike Craig

Lakeside, California
1991–1993 Mickey Thompson
   Off-Road Grand Prix Ultracross Champion

Mike is one of the flashiest riders on the circuit and one of the most talented jumpers. As a former member of Kawasaki's Team Green, he won three consecutive titles during the televised Mickey Thompson Off-Road Grand Prix Series, which also featured truck and ATV racing. Craig later went on to win the 1994 Tampa Supercross.

Ty Davis

Hesperia, California
1987 & 1988 125cc
   CMC Golden State Series Champion
1987 250cc
   CMC Golden State Series Champion
1990 AMA 125cc Western Regional Champion
1991 Four-Stroke National Champion
1993–1995 Baja 1000 Winner
1995 AMA National Reliability
   Enduro Series Champion
1995 Cycle News Rider of the Year
1996 Vegas to Reno Champion
Seven-time ISDE Gold Medalist

In 1999, *Dirt Rider* magazine ranked Ty Davis as the third-greatest rider of all time. As a former motocrosser, he is best known for being the last rider to beat Jeremy McGrath in a Supercross championship. As an off-road racer and a former member of Kawasaki's Team Green, Ty has won nearly every off-road championship plus the legendary Baja 500 and 1000.

John Dowd

Chicopee, Massachusetts

At age 34, John Dowd is the oldest factory rider. His first contract came in 1994 with Yamaha, and he originally signed to ride with that manufacturer before leaving to ride for Team Kawasaki. Dowd earned his coveted ride after winning two 250cc AMA Nationals in 1994 (Millville, Minnesota; and Binghamton, New York) as a privateer.

Danny Hamel

Boulder, Nevada
1992–1995 Hare & Hound Champion
1994 ISDE Medalist
Multi-time Baja 500 & 1000 winner

Before his tragic death during the 1995 Baja 500, Danny was considered the greatest desert racer in the United States. When high speeds were involved, the young Hamel was seemingly unbeatable. He will be greatly missed.

Scot Harden

El Cajon, California
1981 Baja 1000
Multi-time ISDE Medalist
Multi-time Best in the Desert Vet Champion

As the vice president of KTM Sportmotorcycle, Scot is one of the fastest Senior off-road racers in the world. He has earned the number-one plate several times in Best in the Desert competition, and was a member of the 1983 U.S. ISDE Trophy Team.

Steve Hatch

Phoenix, Arizona
1991 International Six Days Enduro
   Junior World Team Champion
1991 AMA Athlete of the Year
1994 AMA National Reliability
   Enduro Champion
Multi-time ISDE Medalist

As a member of the powerful Suzuki factory squad, Steve Hatch has shown his talents throughout the world. He has won several titles and has been a part of Team USA's ISDE effort several years running.

Steve Lamson

Pollock Pines, California
1995 & 1996 AMA 125cc National Champion

Steve Lamson has one of the best work ethics in professional racing. It's that determination that has earned him two National Championships as a member of Team Honda. In 1999, he moved to the 250cc class full time as Jeremy McGrath's teammate in the powerful Chaparral Yamaha camp.

Ron Lechien

El Cajon, California
1984 Unadilla 250cc USGP winner
1985 AMA 125cc
   National Motocross Champion
1989 Hollister 500cc USGP winner

1989 member of the winning Motocross
   des Nations team

Ron is probably the only rider in the world to be born with the same amount of natural talent as Jeremy McGrath. Lechien's smooth technique and near-flawless style has made him a cult figure with diehard race fans. At age 16, Ron became the youngest rider to win a Supercross when he won at Orlando on June 11, 1993. He would go on to win seven more, plus dozens of Nationals.

Jeremy McGrath

San Diego, California
Motocross/Supercross
1993–1996, 1998–1999 Supercross Champion
1995 AMA 250cc National Motocross Champion
1991–1992 AMA 125cc
   West Supercross Champion
1994 member of the winning Motocross
   des Nations team

Hailed as the most natural rider to grace the sport of motocross, Jeremy has won an unprecedented four straight 250 Supercross titles (six if you include his 125cc titles) and won all but one round of the series in the 1996 season while riding for Team Honda. Recently he won back-to-back titles once again in 1998 and 1999. With flawless technique and a habit of getting the holeshot and running away from the pack, Jeremy has dominated the competition like no other rider in the history of the sport. In 1995, he proved those who doubted his outdoor riding ability wrong by wrapping up the 250cc outdoor motocross title. As of press time, he is on his way to another outdoor motocross title and appears to have the ability to win for as long as he cares to ride.

Larry Roeseler

Hesperia, California
1973–1976 AMA District 37 Champion
1989 AMA Hare & Hound 250cc Champion
1991 AMA National Reliability Series Champion
1985 CMC Four-Stroke National Champion
13-time ISDE Medalist
   (10 gold, 2 silver, 1 bronze)
10-time Baja 1000 winner

As a member of Team Husqvarna and Kawasaki's Team Green, Roeseler was the dominant off-road racer in the pre-Ty Davis era. In fact, during Roeseler's career, which spanned more than a decade, he and Davis won Baja several times as teammates.

Rick Sowma

Long Beach, California

Rick has worked as a mechanic for several privateers and even wrenched for Ty Davis part time in 1995. With more than four decades of experience, Sowma has seen it all and is always a great source of knowledge.

Scott Summers

Petersburg, Kentucky

1989 & 1996 International Six Days Enduro
  Gold Medalist
1990, 1992, 1993 & 1994 AMA
  Grand National Cross-Country Champion
1990 AMA Sportsman of the Year
1990, 1991, 1993 & 1995

AMA National Hare & Hound Champion

As Team Honda's most recognizable off-road team, Scott and his mechanic Fred Bramblett are a dominant force in woods racing and have become legendary for putting Honda's XR600 four-stroke into the winner's circle on a regular basis.

About Gary Semics' Absolute Techniques

Gary Semics is the owner and operator of the Gary Semics Motocross School. He trains riders around the country, from beginners to top professionals.

The Gary Semics motocross techniques listed in this book are the result of riding professionally for more than a decade for a number of factory teams, and another decade of teaching motocross at his school. Gary has worked with a variety of riders, ranging from raw novices to one of the smoothest and most precise riders the sport has ever seen—six-time Supercross champ Jeremy McGrath.

The techniques described here, which Gary calls the absolute techniques of motocross, are the basic riding skills needed to excel. They are tailored specifically for motocross, but they apply to all types of off-road motorcycle riding.

Each rider uses his or her own style, but that style comes from these absolute techniques. For example, one rider may find that while cornering he favors the outside line and carries a lot of speed. This is good when you have a clear track, but works less well when you are in a lot of traffic. On the other hand, a different rider may tend to come in hard, brake-slide to turn, and come out hard on the gas. This is good for passing, but requires that you scrub off a lot of speed and need to hook up well to gain it back.

These two riders will both use the absolute techniques, with the difference being how often they choose to use a particular one. The rider carrying a lot of speed, for example, would tend to use a little rear brake to hold a line, while the rider who tends to square off corners would use the front and rear brake to place the front precisely (see Gary Semics' Absolute Techniques: Braking).

The two basic fundamentals of motocross are maintaining the center of balance and mastering the use of all five controls.

Gary Semics (right) is the personal trainer of multi-time champion Jeremy McGrath. The two have worked together since McGrath was an amateur. Here Semics works with McGrath in preseason fitness training.

Semics and McGrath look over some lines on the Yamaha Supercross test track in California.

Maintaining the center of balance deals with body positions and movements. This means that your body positions and movements are always in the right place at the right time. When you have mastered this, the motorcycle will become an extension of your body. You will flow naturally from corner to corner. This is not only the fastest way to ride, it is also typically the most enjoyable and requires less energy.

Mastering the use of all five controls deals with the proper control of the clutch, throttle, front brake, rear brake, and the shifter. When the feeling and precision of these controls are mixed together, the rider has the ultimate control over the motorcycle. The keys here are using several controls at one time, and cutting the transition between braking and accelerating to a minimum.

These basic techniques apply to all aspects of motocross, from corners to whoops to jumps. A good neutral body position is your foundation, and from there you can branch into proper body position while traversing other obstacles. Factor in using the controls, and you have a formula for success for everything from corners to whoops to jumps.

Yes, this book will give you the basic techniques involved in motocross racing, but remember this: The reason the top riders are so fast is because they can perform these techniques better than the rest. These techniques are ingrained into their nervous system, a reflex reaction. Repetition is the mother of skill. The more perfect practice you do, the better you get.

About Gary Semics

Gary Semics was a factory motocross racer for 9 years and has been training riders for more than 15 years as the owner and operator of the Gary Semics School of Motocross. He is better known, however, for his work as the personal trainer for several top riders, including Jeremy McGrath.

Gary is originally from Lisbon, Ohio, where he grew up on his parents' farm. He began racing professionally at age 17. He raced what was then the "Trans-Am" (Trans-America) series, which took him from one end of the country to the other. From 1972 through 1981, Gary was a factory rider for five different manufacturers (Can-Am, Honda, Husqvarna, Kawasaki, and Suzuki). Gary was always a strong contender, finishing consistently in the top ten. Gary won the 1974 500cc Supercross Championship for Husqvarna. He won several Nationals and

placed second and third in the 500 series in 1976 and 1979.

In 1982, Gary began racing the 500cc World Championship Grand Prix. These races featured the best riders in the world competing in just about every country imaginable. His best year was 1982, when he finished a respectable seventh in the 500cc series. After three years of traveling the globe, Semics decided it was time to come home and start a new avenue.

The Gary Semics Motocross School was born in 1985. From there it became Semics' quest to train motocross riders around the country. In order to reach all these motocross enthusiasts, he produced the Gary Semics Motocross Techniques Video Series, which currently includes seven technique videos. He has also produced a historical video entitled *The Evolution of Motocross* and a motocross practice manual.

In 1987, Gary began working with a 16-year-old Jeremy McGrath, who has become a legend of the sport. Gary continues to aid some of the top riders in the world. In addition to being the personal trainer for multi-champion McGrath, he has provided help to other notable riders, including Steve Lamson, Ezra Lusk, Brian Swink, Kyle Lewis, Mike Brown, Branden Jesseman, John Dowd, Kevin Windham, and Ernesto Fonseca.

Chapter 1

How To Choose the Necessities

Off-road motorcycle riding involves a series of calculated risks. Though some are bigger than others, they are all potentially dangerous. Fortunately, aftermarket companies have vastly improved the quality of riding apparel and offer a wide array of high-tech protection equipment. Still, don't be fooled. Even when covered from head to toe in body armor, you can still get hurt.

Safety gear is designed to protect you from minor injury only. There is not a single piece of protective gear on the planet that can offer 100-percent foolproof protection in all situations. Because there is such a wide variety of protective gear on the market, and because the technology changes so rapidly, it is advisable that you do your own research and ask your own questions before making a purchase. Check with your local dealer and ask some of your riding buddies what they have learned about riding gear.

In order to help get you started, this book provides information on some of the key items you should look for.

Helmet

A helmet is perhaps the single most important piece of safety equipment money can buy, and for obvious reasons. Helmets are designed to absorb some of the energy generated during crashes or contact with other objects.

Most manufacturers advise that a helmet should fit snugly so that it doesn't bounce around on your head, but it shouldn't be so tight that it causes discomfort. If you have any questions on sizing or safety issues, it is advisable that you consult the helmet manufacturers directly since they all have their own recommendations and concerns.

Helmets have come a long way from the days when they were open-faced, unvented, and monochromatic. Modern helmets are loaded with features including adjustable visors, ventilation channels, brilliant graphics, goggle strap holders, and removable liners for easy washing. Even though there are too many helmets on the market to list here, several models that are extremely popular among racers and hard-core enthusiasts are worth mentioning.

One of the most popular helmets on the market is Shoei's VFX-R. Though its approximate $400 suggested retail price is on the high end of the scale, many riders find that it's one of the most comfortable helmets because it's also one of the lightest. Like many helmets, the VFX-R features a removable liner and a vented mouthpiece.

Bell also makes several good helmets, including its premier Moto 7 line. Bell helmets are reasonably priced and offer a wide variety of stylish graphics, including some of the hottest racer replicas on the market, among which is the ever-popular McGrath lid. Many riders find that some Moto 7 models feel heavier than some of the competition even though on certain models the weight is comparable. Helmet weight is extremely important, especially in off-road riding, because additional stress on the neck muscles tends to tire and fatigue riders more quickly.

Another inherent characteristic of Bell helmets is a smallish fit. Some riders find that the lining fits snug around the ears and pushes on cheeks. If this is a problem for you, it will be apparent when you try on helmets at your local dealer.

Arai, another major player in the helmet market, has made a name for itself by producing a line of helmets with removable mouth guards. Though most riders use the mouth guard full time, it is common for woods riders to remove the mouthpiece (making it an open-face helmet) to increase airflow. In general, Arai helmets are comfortable and provide a good fit.

Several other companies that produce quality helmets are AXO, Bieffe, Fox, and O'Neal.

While there are dozens of companies producing helmets, this is one area where you shouldn't shop for the best bargain. Also note that there are new helmet regulations in the works, designed to make helmets safer, that will affect the size and shape of helmets in the not-too-distant future.

Finally, always remember that a helmet is designed to be buckled below your chin. It doesn't necessarily have to be tight, but secure enough that the helmet won't accidentally fly off your head while riding or in the event of a crash. It may seem silly, but it happens more than you might think.

In addition to providing protection, most riding gear is also very stylish. Here John Dowd is decked in Fox gear at the Supercross.

GOGGLES

Jeremy McGrath—"Check to make sure that your goggles aren't ripped. If they are, small pieces of debris could get inside and mess up your vision."

Ricky Carmichael—"I always like to have a couple tear-offs just in case. There's really no reason you would ever want to race without having tear-offs ready."

Guy Cooper—"When it's really hot outside I usually attach a panty liner to the upper foam area of my goggles to help absorb sweat. I cut out a one-by-four-inch area near the adhesive area and simply stick it on."

Mike Healey—"When it gets hot I will sometimes wear a bandanna to absorb sweat. This will make sure that drops don't run down my forehead and find their way into my eyes."

Danny Carlson—"When it's really muddy I will make a tear-off to go over a set of Roll-Offs. I super glue the tabs from Scott three-pin tear-offs onto the Roll-Off canisters and then put one or two tear-offs on. Usually the first lap is where you get roosted the most, especially if you have a bad start. By adding the tear-offs, you can insure good vision for a while and still have 30 feet of Roll-Offs to use afterwards."

Steve Lamson—"When you take your goggles to the starting line of any race you should always place them inside a plastic baggie so they don't get dirty."

Rick Sowma—"When it's extremely dusty I sometimes apply a small amount of baby oil to my goggle foam so that dust won't penetrate. This is the same principle as oiling your air filter."

Goggles

Eye protection is vital due to the extreme nature of the sport. Flying rocks, sand and dirt, plus twigs, bushes, and branches can temporarily, and sometimes permanently, blind riders. Additionally, goggles can reduce, and in most cases eliminate, the effect that wind has on the eyes.

How To Set Up Goggles No Matter What the Weather Conditions

Mother Nature can be downright brutal. One minute you can be shredding in loam while the next minute you could be paddling your way through axle-deep mud. Just as bike setup and preparation is determined by weather, so is eye protection. Without proper vision you simply cannot ride with confidence and total control. Restricted vision can slow you down and no vision stops you dead in your tracks.

While most people believe that goggle prep is as simple as cleaning the lens, they frequently overlook the multitude of variables and options. The truth is that there are literally hundreds of combinations to consider when you enter the world of Turbofans, tear-offs, Roll-Offs, frame choice, lens selection, and so on. The best way to determine what works best for you is to experiment. Either borrow what you don't have from your friends or go to your local dealership and buy a supply of goggle accessories you think might be beneficial and then try some different combinations.

Frame Choice

There are many different goggle frames available: children's goggles, adult goggles, and over-the-glasses goggles. Regardless of what brand, style, or size you choose, you need to make sure that the goggles fit comfortably inside your helmet and provide you with adequate peripheral vision. Additionally, it's important that your goggles fit your face because facial features will affect comfort and the ability of the goggles to keep debris from entering inside the sealed chamber. Also, it's vital that you make sure your goggles fit inside your helmet. Eyeport sizes vary wildly among the helmet manufacturers and therefore must be taken into consideration. For example, Smith's original Violator does not easily fit into some helmet models such as the popular line made by Bieffe.

Lens Selection

Goggle manufacturers sell a variety of lenses designed for all types of weather conditions. Lens designs range from colored lenses, which help with lighting conditions, to thicker lenses, which reduce fogging. These are the most common lenses used:

CLEAR: The most popular lens and the only lens that goggle manufacturers suggest using for all types of riding.

GRAY OR SMOKE: Recommended by Scott U.S.A., Smith Sport Optics, and Oakley for bright sun.

ORANGE: Recommended by Smith Sport Optics for overcast/muddy, overcast/dusty, and rainy conditions.

YELLOW: Recommended by Smith Sport Optics for overcast/muddy, overcast/dusty, and rainy conditions. Smith also suggests that a yellow lens should be a serious option for riding at night.

GRADIENT: A clear lens with a narrow band of smoke or gray at the top. This lens works like a bifocal for riding in bright conditions. In the normal position the lens is clear, but when you tilt your head down it appears either gray or smoke, depending on the particular lens.

Goggle frames come in a wide variety of shapes and sizes, from over-the-glasses goggles to children's goggles. The most important considerations are that the goggles fit comfortably inside your helmet and provide you with adequate peripheral vision.

An assortment of different goggle lenses are available, ranging from colored lenses for different lighting conditions to no-fog lenses.

Vision is what goggles are all about, and a large dollop of roost deposited on your lenses is all it takes to blind a rider. The solution is to (A) holeshot every race or (B) get some tear-offs or Roll-Offs. Tear-offs (a peel-off film) clear the entire goggle but only wipe your vision five to ten times. Roll-Offs (shown) give you 30 feet of film to work with, but only clear a strip of vision.

MIRROR: Used mostly in dusty conditions encountered in bright skies.

DOUBLE-PANE: Two clear lenses bonded together that reduce fogging. Double-pane lenses come in a variety of colors to suit your needs.

FOG-RESISTANT: A single-pane lens with small holes drilled around the edges to allow air flow. The holes are covered with a mi-cro-fiber cloth intended to keep debris out of the eye port.

Face Masks

Face masks gained a lot of popularity in the early 1980s before full-face helmets were common. Originally face masks attached to the goggle and extended to chin level to protect a rider's face from flying objects. Though most goggle companies still sell full masks, for those riders who prefer open-face helmets, a smaller version known as a half-mask, which covers a rider's upper lip, is available. The half-mask is preferred for full-face helmets, especially on rocky courses.

Tear-Offs and Film Systems

When moisture is present, it often obstructs clear vision. Take mud, for example: One good douse of roost and your goggles are wasted. Tear-offs and Roll-Offs, however, were designed to combat this vision problem. Though tear-offs and Roll-Offs work differently, they both operate on the same principle: Cover the goggle lens with an ultra-thin piece of plastic film that is discarded when vision is obstructed. Tear-offs consist of one or more (up to 10, depending on the manufacturer) sheets of film secured on top of the goggle lens. When a rider needs to clear the lens, he/she can take his/her left hand off the handlebar, grab the tab attached to the tear-off, and simply pull it away from the goggle—hence the name tear-off.

Smith's Roll-Offs work in a similar fashion but do not clear the entire field of vision. Instead, Roll-Offs use a 1 1/4-inch-wide strip of film that clears debris. The system stores roughly 30 feet of new film in a weather-resistant canister on the right side of the lens (also known as the supply side). Opposite is a take-up spool connected to a small spring-loaded cord. When the string is pulled, the system advances film across the front of the goggle. The advantage is that Roll-Offs are equivalent to roughly 25 to 30 tear-offs. The drawback is that it only clears a thin band across the lens.

If you use Roll-Offs, make sure you use Smith's Roll-Off visor. This adhesive-backed plastic strip lies directly beneath the upper rim of the goggle and prevents dust, dirt, and mud from getting trapped between the film and the lens surface.

The Prescription Alternative

A California-based company called Pro-Vue modifies goggles to accept prescription lenses for certain types of eye corrections. Pro-Vue's system will work with most major brands of goggles as well as with tear-offs and Smith Roll-Offs. Pro-Vue, 357 Sandy Point Court NE, Rochester, MN 55906, 800/548-8354.

Water and Dust Repellents and No-Fog Cloths

When your riding plans run into rain, an automotive product called Rain-X could turn out to be your best friend. When applied to the exterior of a goggle lens it disperses rain, sleet, and snow for hours on end. You can order Rain-X direct or find it in most places that sell automotive supplies. Rain-X, 7428 East Karen Drive, Scottsdale, AZ 85260, 800/542-6424.

Like water, dust is one of the most difficult elements to deal with because it gets everywhere. The most effective way to cope with dust is to use a repellent such as Mr. Moto Quick Polish. The solution is sprayed on and then buffed out using a lens cloth. It's recommended that you apply Quick Polish to both sides of the goggle lens in case dust penetrates the goggle foam.

Another lens treatment is a no-fog cloth. Just as the name implies, a no-fog cloth is a chemically treated cloth designed to reduce the effects of fogging. The cloth, which is used to coat the interior and exterior of the lens, can also double as a lens cleaner.

Modular Goggle System

Smith Sport Optics may have paved the way for the future of goggles with the creation of the Violator. The Violator is a goggle that totally comes apart, allowing a rider to either utilize the foam or remove it for cold-weather situations where dust isn't present. The kit comes with two foam densities for use with different dust and temperature conditions. The Violator also has exterior Roll-Off mounts so the film canisters don't have to be mounted on the lens, as in the original method of Roll-Off placement.

Gloves

Since your hands operate most of the controls (such as the throttle, clutch, and front brake), it is critical that you choose gloves that you feel absolutely comfortable wearing. In general, gloves should fit snugly but not be so tight that they feel restrictive, es-pecially in the web area at the base of your fingers. It is also important that your gloves are not too big; otherwise, the excess material will reduce your sensitivity and ability to operate the controls. You should also make sure that your gloves seal properly around your cuffs to keep debris from entering but not so tightly that they will cause arm pump. Some gloves have hook-and-loop straps around the cuffs, which are excellent, but they are often fastened too tightly by anxious riders.

If you purchase gloves designed for off-road motorcycle riding, you should try on several brands. Motorcycle gloves have additional padding in the palms and usually a second layer of material on top of the hand. Depending on the quantity of padding and the type of material, some glove styles will be more comfortable than others.

Additionally, most manufacturers produce a lighter-weight glove for mud use. The gloves are made mostly of cotton and have small rubber beads in the palm area that provide additional traction.

Jersey

Most motocross and off-road riders wear their jerseys a little loose so movement is not restricted. Most jerseys are made out of cotton, but some companies, such as MSR, have been experimenting with breathable waterproof materials that should already be at dealerships by now.

Regardless of the material, some riders stretch out the cuffs on their wrists because the elasticity can sometimes hinder circulation, which has been linked to arm pump. Some riders, like Ron Lechien, cut off the elastic part of the cuffs.

If the cost of a new $30 to $60 jersey is a deterrent, you may consider checking to see if your dealer has any older gear in stock that is for sale at a reduced price. Some companies, like Fox Racing, also offer a budget clothing line that still looks stylish and, in many cases, provides the exact same fit as the much more expensive line.

Kidney Belt

A kidney belt is extremely important because it provides much-needed lower back support and because it helps keep internal organs in place. Kidney belts should be worn fairly snug around the waist, on top of the jersey but underneath the pants.

	LENS						SET UP							
---	CLEAR	SMOKE	ORANGE	YELLOW	GRADIENT	MIRROR	TEAR-OFFS (no.)	ROLL-OFFS	TEAR-OFF/ROLL-OFF	NO-FOG	RAIN X	ANTI-STATIC	FOAM OIL	HALF-MASK
BRIGHT SUN	R	R			R	R	6	O	O	R		O		O
BRIGHT SUN/DUSTY	R	R					3	O	O	R			R	O
BRIGHT SUN/MUDDY	R	R					6	R	R	R	O			O
OVERCAST	R		O	O			6	O	O	R			O	O
OVERCAST/DUSTY	R		O	O		R	3	O	O	R		O	R	O
OVERCAST/MUDDY	R		O	O			4	R	O	R	O			O
NIGHT	R		O	O			4	O	O	R				O
RAIN	R		O	O				R	R	R	R			O
KEY							R = Recommended		O = Optional					

When buying a kidney belt, don't assume that they are all the same just because they look a lot alike. Kidney belts come in all shapes and sizes and are made out of all sorts of materials; some are even reinforced with plastic. Try on a variety of kidney belts at your dealer to see what feels comfortable, and when you're doing this, make sure you try them on with your chest protector, because sometimes the two will interfere with one another.

Chest Protector

A chest protector is designed to shield the rider from roost thrown up by other riders. Though chest protectors that come with shoulder pads may also help protect the shoulders, most manufacturers do not make any claims as to the effectiveness of shoulder protection.

Chest protectors come in a variety of sizes and offer a wide range of protection. Ideally, when choosing a chest protector you want to find adequate protection that doesn't restrict mobility beyond your liking.

Furthermore, Acerbis makes a chest protector, called the Zoom, that has plastic guards near the kidney area on each side that provide additional coverage. Acerbis also

manufactures a unique chest protector for women called the Lady Proton.

In addition to normal chest protectors that cover the front and back of a rider's upper torso, some companies manufacture chest protectors that protect the front exclusively. It's also common to find chest protectors on the market that have a modular design (such as Answer, AXO, and Malcolm Smith), which allow biceps guards and back panels to be removed.

Riding Pants

In the sport's beginning, riding pants were constructed purely of leather because it was the most durable material available. Over time, however, leather became too expensive (not to mention too hot in the summer), which pushed clothing companies to seek out a variety of alternative materials, including synthetics, to create more realistically priced riding apparel.

Since the late 1970s, most pants have been constructed of nylon with polyester linings, and have featured removable hip pads and knee cups that provide additional protection. Though the features are usually identical or very similar among the

dozen or so manufacturers, sizing and cut is another story.

Make sure you try on any pants you intend to purchase. Be sure that there is enough room in the thighs, knees, and groin. You don't want the pants too loose, but you don't want them too tight, either. Essentially, you don't want them to restrict your movement.

Among the apparel manufacturers, there is a wide range of patterns that affect sizing, so make sure you look at all of your options.

Pricing varies wildly from $100 to $200 depending on style, size, and brand name. While most pants hover in the $170 range, both Fox Racing and MSR produce two lines of pants on opposite ends of the price spectrum. Typically, the less expensive pants have fewer sewn-on graphics and are more generic, but offer virtually identical protection as the more expensive kind.

One of the most important things to look for when buying pants is double-stitching. It is also advisable to be very careful when looking over any pair of pants you intend to buy. Though quality control is excellent, every once in a while you may find a pair of pants that has been cut improperly or has irregular sewing.

Knee Braces or Knee Pads

For knee protection, you have two choices: the knee and shin cups that come with most leathers, or a knee brace. There are a variety of knee braces on the market that will fit most budgets, and they are becoming increasingly popular. Some knee braces may even be covered under your medical insurance if you have had a knee injury, so check with them before laying out any of your own cash.

If you plan to use a knee brace instead of the traditional knee cups, you should be aware that they may not fit comfortably in all leathers. Some pants fit tightly around the knee; therefore, when buying new pants you should take your knee braces to your favorite motorcycle shop and try on leathers with your knee braces. Some riders, like McGrath, also cut the lining out of their leathers so that the knee braces are less restricted. Riders who wear knee braces also wear an amputee-style sock beneath their knee brace(s) to minimize chafing. There are a dozen or so companies that offer knee

A growing number of top riders have elected to cut the linings out of their riding pants to provide less restriction, especially when knee braces are worn. Riders who do so usually wear a pair of bicycle-type shorts underneath. Several motorcycle apparel companies such as Xtreme and MSR make the shorts without all of the extra padding in the crotch found in bicycle shorts.

Knee braces, like this CTi2 made by Innovation Sports (shown on Danny Carlson with the optional patella or knee cup), are one of the more popular trends in protective equipment. The CTi2, worn by riders such as Jeremy McGrath, Damon Bradshaw, Doug Henry, Larry Roeseler, Guy Cooper, Jeff Emig, and Steve Lamson, is a custom-made knee brace manufactured out of carbon fiber and titanium. Innovation Sports also sells an off-the-shelf knee brace known as The Edge.

braces designed for motocross and other high-risk sports. Custom-fit and off-the-shelf models are both available.

Boots

A good pair of boots is essential because the foot and ankle take a lot of abuse. This is one item where it pays not to be cheap.

One of the most popular models is Alpinestars' Tech-7, because of its excellent break-in and wear characteristics. Alpinestars boots are so popular that entire companies, like MSR, have their boots produced by the famed Italian company.

Sidi's Top Action Evolution 2 is also an excellent choice of footwear because it provides a good fit and lasts a fairly long time. Sidi also makes a more expensive version (about $20 more) called the Sole Replacement System (SRS) that allows the soles to be changed once they get worn out from grinding on the footpegs.

You may also want to consider adding an insole, which will make the boots more comfortable and also lessen some of the impact of hard landings.

Socks

Most riders wear a pair of thick cotton tube socks that cover the entire calf. This reduces chafing that would normally result from wearing an ankle-high sock. Thick socks seem a bit odd in the heat of summer, but they are essential to keeping your feet dry and cushioned. Off-road boots are incredibly durable and allow you to be confident that your feet and ankles can comfortably withstand a beating, but because the boots are incredibly tough, they are also stiff and unyielding when compared to tennis shoes or other daily footwear, which can be rough on your feet and calves.

Some of today's high-tech fabrics can be helpful, especially for winter riding. Look for socks that are polypropylene lined, as they will wick moisture away from your feet. This is especially important for long rides, when your feet will be in the boots for half a day or more. You can also use thin polypropylene socks as a liner for heavier socks.

Some riders place insoles into their boots to help provide a little extra cushion on hard landings. Insoles usually cost around $15 and simply slip into the boot.

Off-road riders will find that off-road jackets serve a variety of vital functions. Most important, they offer protection from the elements such as chilly temperatures, rain, and snow. Most are made out of water-resistant materials and do an excellent job of keeping the rider dry, yet also feature breather holes so the rider doesn't overheat.

Enduro Jacket

Off-road jackets are a great way to keep the weather away in cooler or rainy conditions. Gore-Tex is ideal for off-road riding because it breathes and allows sweat to evaporate while keeping you dry when doused with rain or snow.

Controlling body temperature is extremely critical when riding. Less-experienced riders tend to dress too warmly and forget that their body will warm up naturally while riding. Hence, it is not uncommon to see riders with entirely too many layers of clothing. Though they will be warm, their movements will be restricted to the point that it may slow their reflexes.

Because temperature is such a critical factor, some companies specialize in producing enduro jackets with removable sleeves. This allows the jacket to be instantly converted into a vest.

Fanny packs are a necessity for off-road riding, regardless of whether it's trail riding or racing. The tools and spare parts stored inside are often your only means of making repairs on the trail. Also note that most motorcycle shops carry a wide variety of lightweight multi-use tools to save space.

Enduro jackets also offer plenty of storage space for maps, spare parts, snacks, and many items needed on the trail.

Fanny Packs

Fanny packs are a necessity for off-road riding regardless of whether you are trail riding or racing. The tools and spare parts stored inside are often your only means of making repairs on the trail. The most important aspect is making sure you have enough parts but not so many that the pack becomes too heavy to carry. Secondly, make sure the items inside don't bounce around, because it can be very annoying. If the items are bouncing around, a simple cure is to fill up the space with a shop rag. The rag may also come in very handy on the trail.

When wearing a fanny pack it is very important to wear it snugly around the waist. You don't want to have it be too loose; otherwise, it will flop all over the place while you ride. Items typically carried in a fanny pack are: Phillips and slot-head screwdrivers, wire cutters, spark plug(s) and spark plug wrench, pliers, 8-, 10-, and 12mm wrenches and sockets, knife, Zip-ties, electrical tape, safety wire, master link, and a small assortment of nuts and bolts. Many tools can be found in combination form to consolidate packing.

How To Dress for Temperature and Conditions

Inevitably you are going to come across difficult weather—be it cold or warm

Even when the weather is cool, drink systems are important on long rides. Most, like this one on the back of Guy Cooper, are carried on the back and hold several quarts of fluid. Some riders carry bicycle-type squeeze bottles on the sides of their fanny packs.

weather, or even stormy conditions—that will force you to make a well-calculated decision on what to wear.

Typically, warm weather is the easiest to judge, because you can't strip down any further than the bare essentials. Some riders, however, wear vented jerseys or cut 100 or so one- to two-inch slots on their jerseys using normal household scissors.

Another way to stay cool is to carry water in either a backpack-style carrier or hip-mounted bicycle-type squeeze bottle.

In sharp contrast, proper cold weather apparel is much more difficult to select. The trick is putting on enough clothing to keep you warm but not so much that you immediately become drenched in sweat (dampness makes you cold and miserable for the rest of the ride).

The ultimate goal when staying warm is to stay dry, and there are really two basic keys to staying dry in cold weather: layering and high-tech fabrics. If you dress in layers, you can peel off clothing as you warm up. If you are on the trail, a large buttpack or backpack can serve as a place to store clothing as you take it off.

Layering T-shirts and sweatshirts will get you by, but you'll still get wet with sweat and then get cold when you stop. Modern fabrics are the other, more important, part of the equation. Fabrics like Gore-Tex make an ideal outer layer because they prevent you from getting soaked with snow roost yet allow sweat to pass through them. The inner layer should be polypropylene or something similar, as these materials wick sweat away from your body, keeping you dry underneath. The combination turns cold weather riding into a roost-fest of long power slides that make you feel like Scotty Parker.

By adding the following items to your regular riding gear, you can stay comfortable in a wide variety of cold temperatures. High-tech fabrics allow you to get by with just poly underwear and a Gore-Tex jersey on 20-degree and above days. Keep in mind that you'll cool off if you stop, so you should carry more clothing for a trail ride.

1. Polypropylene long underwear (top and bottom)
2. Long-sleeved turtleneck (optional)
3. Gore-Tex jersey
4. Gore-Tex riding pants (spray your regular riding pants with 3M Scotchguard or other water-repellent for a cheap substitute)
5. Polypropylene sock liners
6. Heavy wool socks
7. Glove liners such as those made by UnderWARE
8. Enduro jacket (preferably Gore-Tex, with removable sleeves)

Gore-Tex clothing isn't cheap, but it makes an enormous difference when riding during the winter and is durable enough to last you a lifetime. Gore-Tex clothing is also ideal for riding in rain, obviously. When there is threat of moisture, most riders use an MSR Pak-Jak in mild temperatures or a Gore-Tex enduro jacket when it's a bit cooler. These are combined with either normal nylon riding pants or a Gore-Tex pant like MSR's Pak-Pant. You can find the poly long underwear, socks, and glove liners at a good outdoor store for a reasonable price.

Chapter 2

MOTORCYCLE SETUP TIPS

The Most Critical Time You Can Spend with Your Bike

Over the last decade, motorcycle setup has become increasingly important as technology continues to develop at an astounding rate. In addition to scheduled maintenance, a motorcycle must be set up properly for each particular rider. Everything from rider height, weight, style, and ability factor into the ever-developing formula of motorcycle setup. This information, combined with other variables such as track and weather conditions and the type of motorcycle, results in a number of setup combinations and variables impossible to count.

The place to begin is fitting the motorcycle to the rider. When riding well, an off-road bike becomes an extension of the rider's body. The two function as a unit, flowing with the terrain rather than fighting it. For this to happen, the motorcycle needs to fit the rider like a glove.

It's also very important to realize that motorcycle setup isn't a one-time job. Since there are so many variables, setup will change on a daily and sometimes an hourly basis, even if you are riding at the same place in the same conditions. For this reason, it is recommended that you maintain a motorcycle setup log so you can keep track of what works and what doesn't. Here is a description of the most common starting points for developing your own personal preference.

Handlebar

The handlebar may be one of the most important setup items because it single-hand-

Proper motorcycle setup is an absolute must, because it determines how well your motorcycle will work and ultimately how much fun you can have. This photo of Guy Cooper inside his race shop in Stillwater, Oklahoma, illustrates proper clutch and brake lever positioning. Notice that when Cooper's arms are in the attack position, the levers are almost on the same angle, just a little lower. This will serve as a good starting point for you to determine your personal preference.

edly dictates how a rider will be able to move around on the motorcycle. The aftermarket offers bars with a wide variety of heights and sweep.

In general, taller riders will usually prefer a taller handlebar while those vertically challenged will appreciate a lower bar. You may find that this doesn't apply to you, though.

Riders tend to have different tastes, so try a few different bars to discover what suits you.

One way to get an idea of what works best for you is by loosening the bar clamps and rotating the bar on your bike out of the way. Then sit on the seat with the bike on the stand and get into your standard body position. Close your eyes and imagine reaching

Jeremy McGrath is one of the best riders at setting up his machinery, and that's one of the many reasons why his riding style looks so effortless.

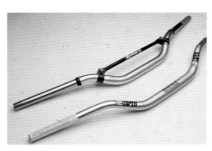

The latest trend in ultra-strong handlebars is an oversized lower tube. Renthal's Twinwall (above) and Answer's ProTaper (below) are arguably the strongest bars ever developed. Unfortunately, they also require the use of an oversized upper bar clamp and sometimes an entirely new upper tripleclamp.

out and grabbing the handlebar. The imaginary bar is very close to ideal for you. Now match a real bar to the bar you visualized.

Next, rotate the bar back up and snug the bolts finger tight. Get into your standard body position again, close your eyes, and reach for the bars. You may find that the point you visualized earlier and the actual location of the bars are different. Adjust the bars, getting as close as possible to the bar you visualized. If the bar you are using can't be adjusted to that point, you should try a different bar. This should give you an idea of how the bar should vary from the bar you are using. Ideally, take your old bar to the shop and compare it to new models. By comparing the two, you should be able to find a bar that suits your needs (a bit higher/lower, a little more sweep back, etc.).

Keep in mind that your standard body position will affect which bar you prefer. As your riding skills improve, so will your body position, so you should periodically check how your bars fit and make the proper adjustments.

Regardless of which bend you like, an aluminum handlebar is preferable because of the strength. Steel bars are cheaper, but they also bend easily. Aluminum bars, especially the better-quality units, are amazingly strong and will justify the extra expense after a few simple get-offs. Among conventional handlebars, Renthal bars make one of the most popular lines, one that has been race-tested by many World and National Champions.

Safety wire is a key ingredient for serious racers. Typically, it's used to double-lock trips and key fasteners.

A unique and perhaps the strongest line is the ProTaper sold by Answer Products. Pro-Taper bars have no crossbar and (as the name suggests) are tapered and are much wider where the handlebar connects to the upper triple clamp. ProTapers are costly, at almost $100 a set, and that doesn't include the hardware required to accept the thicker handlebar. If your bike has removable bar clamps

you may get away with spending about $50 for the extra parts, but if your machine has a solid clamp, it could cost you as much as $150. However, the bar will pay for itself in the long run if you are the type who normally bends handlebars easily.

Width is another way to tailor your bars to your needs. While motocrossers and desert racers usually prefer to use the stock width (usually around 30 to 31 inches), cross-country and enduro riders tend to shorten the bars to 28 or 29 inches to give the bike a narrower profile so that it can fit between trees much easier. Please note that the narrower the handlebar, the less control you will have over the bike because of the decreased leverage.

Once you have decided the type of handlebar and the width, the bar should be centered on the motorcycle and then you should sit on the bike to determine the angle of the handlebar before tightening the clamp bolts. Typically, most riders prefer to run their handlebar so that the bar ends are parallel to the ground. However, some riders, like motocrosser Larry Ward, run their handlebars way up.

This upper tripleclamp has removable bar clamps that will accept oversize bars such as Twinwalls and ProTapers. The clamps themselves are also reversible so riders can change the distance between the bars and the rider. Some companies even sell clamps that are shorter and taller to give riders a wider range of customization.

Triple Clamp

Beginning in the 1990s, the aftermarket has offered triple clamps that change the location of the handlebar mount. This allows a rider to relocate the handlebar either closer to or farther away from the rider and, in some cases, can also raise handlebar height. Some motorcycles already come stock with rubber-mounted bar clamps that can be rotated 180 degrees to change the distance of the handlebar to the rider. Most changes are very minor but this is a way to fine-tune handling.

Because triple clamp height can be so important, motocrosser Larry Ward reportedly had several custom sets of upper clamps made in 1mm increments so that he can change from track to track. Several companies build triple clamps; one of the most common brands is Applied Racing.

Handlebar Grips

There are dozens of different handlebar grips available and preferences vary wildly. To prevent blisters, some riders choose to shave several rows of ribs off the top of the grip (this is not advisable when riding in wet conditions because it will reduce traction). Motocrossers usually tend to run a softer compound while off-road riders tend to use harder compounds because of their excellent wear characteristics.

Grips should be glued to the handlebar using a grip glue and then safety wired to the handlebar to reduce the chances of a grip spinning and coming loose.

Levers

The clutch and front brake levers need to be easily accessible to the rider while both sitting and standing. If the levers are too high, they will be difficult to use when standing. Conversely, if the levers are too low, they will be difficult to use when sitting.

As a starting point, most riders sit on their bike with both perches loose enough to spin with minimal pressure. The levers should be positioned at the same angle as the rider's arms when sitting in the attack position, and then tightened to the manufacturer's recommended specifications. When in your standard riding position, your fingers should rest naturally on the levers. When your elbows are positioned correctly (slightly high), the levers will be pivoted forward. Be sure to assume a good body position when setting the levers.

Also, position the levers so that the end of the bar is about 3/8 of an inch away from the end of the handlebar. This will decrease the likelihood of a lever snapping during a crash.

A Honda clutch lever and perch from a newer CR125 or CR250R work well for any brand. The Honda perches offer the closest thing to a perfect leverage ratio and can be adapted to fit most motocross and off-road bikes.

Seat

The seat is another part of the motorcycle that can be tailored to the rider, either with different seat covers or by modifying the foam. Though many riders stick with the stock seat, the aftermarket does make different foam densities that you should be aware of. There are also seat covers available with a built-in gripping system that helps eliminate any unwanted sliding around on the seat. The grippier seat is especially useful when gripping the seat with your knees, a critical aspect of riding, especially in motocross.

If you are taller than average or suffer from knee problems, you may consider building yourself a taller seat using scraps of seat foam. Conversely, some shorter riders cut down their seats by carefully using a coarse kitchen knife. In fact, many Supercross riders also shorten the front of their seats so that they can get better body positioning in the corners. You have to watch out, though. If you shave too much off your seat you will find that your butt will get pounded against the plastic seat base, which can be quite painful.

Shift Lever

Adjusting the location of the shift lever is another important alteration you can make to tailor the bike to you.

The lever can be moved in small increments thanks to multiple splines on the shift shaft. Aftermarket shifters sometimes have different bends than the stock levers, and are more economical than factory pieces. The aftermarket models are typically steel, as well, which is slightly heavier but much more durable than the stock aluminum shifters.

Grips come in a variety of shapes, sizes, and rubber types. Since they only cost $10 to $15 and are the link to the most important set of controls, it's recommended that you experiment to find out what works best for you.

The clutch and brake levers should be positioned approximately 3/8 inch away from the end of the handlebar. This will help minimize the chances of the levers breaking during a crash. The best way to measure is to pull the lever as close to the grip as possible.

As a starting point, most riders position the shift lever so the bottom is parallel with the top of the footpeg.

Though opinions vary, most riders prefer to adjust the rear brake pedal height so that it is even with the footpeg.

In general, adjust the shifter so that the bottom of the lever is on the same horizontal plane as the top of the footpeg. You may find that you prefer it a bit higher or lower, but keep in mind that you have to be able to shift from a sitting or standing position.

Brake Pedal

The location of the brake pedal is just as important as that of the shift lever. As a starting point, most riders will adjust their brake pedal (in the resting position) so that the top of the actual pedal lies on the same horizontal plane as the footpegs. From there,

tailor it subtly so you can use the pedal when sitting or standing. Once adjustment is complete, make sure the rear brake doesn't drag. Keep in mind that brakes can drag when they are hot, so be sure and get the brakes good and warm (take a few laps using the rear brake hard) and then double-check that they aren't dragging.

Tires

If you've ever watched a NASCAR race, then you are probably keenly aware of the important role that tires play in motorsports. Though many factory-backed riders use tires

with special compounds, the tire manufacturers have done an excellent job of producing off-the-shelf tires for a wide variety of conditions. Usually the best way to determine which tire will work best in your type of terrain is to see what other serious riders are using. The choice is always a matter of opinion, and even the tire manufacturers aren't always sure which will work best on a particular type of terrain.

No matter what the conditions, a worn-out tire will give you bad results. Once the sharp edges of the knobs round off, grip is lost. Top pros use a fresh set of tires for every moto; you'll have to make your own decision on how often to change tires. You can lengthen tire life a bit by flipping it on the rim, but braking effect will be lessened. Front tires typically last much longer than the rears, and different conditions are harder on tires than others. Just keep in mind that when the knobs get rounded off, you are losing traction.

Most tires are designed to run air pressure between 12 and 15 psi. The lower the air pressure, the better the traction, but also the more vulnerable the inner tube is to flats.

One way to reduce flats altogether is to install a solid foam insert known as a bib mousse. Michelin and Moose Racing both make these special puncture-proof bib mousses that cost between $100 and $130, and Dunlop is also producing a foam insert with a miniature inner tube inside.

Unfortunately, bib mousses are extremely difficult to install (requiring special tools and lubricants) and also wear out fairly rapidly. While the manufacturers are working on ways to increase the life, the compounds break down with abuse and excess heat.

Bib mousses feel different from inner tubes because they have different shock-absorbing characteristics. That is precisely why Dunlop has created the mousse that uses the small inflatable inner tube so that the sensitivity can be controlled.

Suspension

Suspension setup is the most critical element of motorcycle setup. Spring rate, oil levels, internal valving, rebound and compression damping settings, preload, sag, and especially motorcycle type, can make all the difference in the world as to how a bike handles. Due to the extreme complexity involved, we must refer you to your owners

Tire choice is extremely critical and must be taken seriously. While there are many tire manufacturers, typically Bridgestone, Dunlop, Metzeler, Michelin, and Pirelli make the best products on the market. While it is key to use a compound and tread pattern that match conditions, it is more important to have fresh rubber on your bike. When the knobs round off, you are getting less than optimum traction.

Oversize rotors gained popularity during the early 1990s as a way to increase brake power. Oversize kits usually include the rotor, a backing plate, and new brake pads, and sell for about $250.

manual or to the book *Motocross and Off-Road Motorcycle Performance Handbook* (see appendix for details) for guidelines, because an entire book can be written on suspension setup alone.

PRO SETUP TIPS
BIKE SETUP

Jeremy McGrath—"I spend a lot of time testing different [external] gear ratios. It's amazing what kind of difference one tooth on the rear sprocket makes. Without proper gearing, your bike will never reach its fullest potential because you'll constantly find yourself compensating with your riding style. When a bike isn't properly geared, you'll usually notice that you're constantly between gears and using too much clutch."

Steve Lamson—"It's really important to make sure that your brakes are working properly. I find it necessary to bleed the brake lines frequently to avoid a mushy feel."

Mike Craig—"Installing new cables or lubing old ones is a must. I find that I get less arm pump when clutch pull is easy."

John Dowd—"Replace your clutch perch and lever when it develops slop up and down. This is one good way to keep your bike feeling fresh."

Mike Healey—"When I'm setting up a new bike I always experiment with different handlebar bends. I want something that complements the ergonomics of the motorcycle. In general, I usually pick what feels most natural."

Ty Davis—"For off-road I use a braided front brake line. It's extremely powerful because it has less flex than the conventional plastic lines."

Mike Healey—"I install beefed-up footpegs on all of my bikes. I like the wider feel, plus I don't want to worry about a bent footpeg ruining my day."

Ty Davis—"When riding tight, slippery trails, I use a heavier flywheel. The added weight alters the power characteristics by not allowing the engine to rev as fast as normal. This produces less wheelspin and enables me to stay hooked up."

Mike Kiedrowski—"For more stopping power I use an oversize front brake rotor."

Serious recreational riders and racers will usually have their suspension set up by an aftermarket company before fine-tuning it in the field. If you decide to have your suspension modified, check with other riders to see which aftermarket companies are doing the best work for your type of bike. There are hundreds of suspension companies scattered throughout the United States, and each has its own opinion of what works and what doesn't.

Fork Tube Height

On the average, most riders raise their fork about 5–10mm in the triple clamp. For quicker turning the tubes can be raised even

A wide variety of guards is available to protect motorcycles against abuse. This engine guard is designed for off-road use and protects the engine cases, lower frame rails, and water pump cover. Notice that there is a small hole in the bottom to allow gear oil to be changed easily.

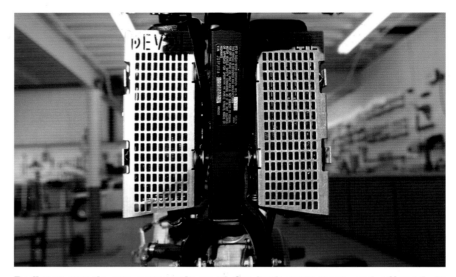

Radiator guards are commonly used for both motocross and off-road. In addition to protecting the radiator from flying debris, the framework of the guards actually makes the entire radiator stronger and less susceptible to bending. A new radiator sells for $200 or more. A pair of guards go for about $80. You do the math.

farther (until they hit the base of the handlebar). The drawback is that this will decrease high-speed stability and may cause head-shake. Conversely, lowering the fork tubes to the point where the upper tube is flush with the top of the upper triple clamp will give you greater high-speed stability at the sacrifice of turning ability.

Guards

There are several different types of guards designed to protect your motorcycle from impact damage. Typically, motocrossers do not require as much armor as off-road riders, but most of these pieces are useful for any kind of riding. It can't hurt to protect parts of your motorcycle.

Skid Plate
(motocross and off-road)

The most common type is a glide plate, which is a flat aluminum plate that protects the bottom of the engine and most of the frame rails. Larger versions that wrap around the frame rails and protect the water pump cover or even the exhaust pipe are also available. Off-road riders typically use the larger skid plates, while motocross racers favor the trim, light glide plates.

Pipe Guard
(primarily off-road)

A plastic or metal guard that wraps around the front, lower section of the exhaust pipe to keep it from getting dented.

Frame Guard
(motocross and off-road)

Protects lower portions of the frame near the swingarm pivot bolt. The right side unit also protects the rear brake master cylinder from minor damage. These will keep paint from wearing off your frame. When combined with a skid plate, they can lengthen the life of your frame.

Front Master Cylinder Guard
(motocross and off-road)

A small aluminum guard that protects the front master cylinder. Compare the cost of these guards to that of a new master cylinder and you'll see why they are useful.

Radiator Guards
(primarily off-road, becoming more popular among motocrossers)

Dual aluminum vented plates designed to keep rocks, branches, and other objects from damaging ultra-expensive radiators. A Washington-based company, DeVol, goes a step further than most other companies by

adding support braces on the sides to provide additional impact protection.

Bark Busters
(woods riders)

A metal guard that protects the hands from impact damage caused by trees. The guards also make the handlebar more sturdy.

Hand Guards
(off-road riders or anyone riding in cold or muddy conditions)

Plastic shields that protect the hands from flying debris such as rocks and mud. In cold weather, they also keep hands warm. Some companies also sell an optional spoiler kit that shields your hands a bit better.

Disc Guard
(motocross and off-road riders)

Usually made of plastic, but sometimes constructed of aluminum, a disc guard is designed to keep the rotors from getting pitted or dinged. Disc guards are so important that some manufacturers include disc guards on production machinery.

Shark Fin
(primarily off-road riders)

A solid piece of metal, usually aluminum, that protects the rear brake rotor from impact damage.

MOTORCYCLE SETUP CHART

GENERAL DATA

Date:_____ Location:_____ Air temperature:_____ Humidity:_____Elevation:_____

Description of terrain and conditions:_____

SUSPENSION

Fork spring rate:_____ Fork oil level:_____ Fork compression (number of turns out):_____

Fork rebound damping (number of turns out):_____

Fork tube height (distance from top of fork tube to triple clamp):_____

Shock spring rate:_____

Shock low-speed compression (number of turns out):_____

Shock high-speed compression (number of turns out):_____

Shock rebound damping (number of turns out):_____

Shock sag:_____ Shock preload:_____

CHASSIS

Handlebar type: _____ Handlebar bend: _____

Handlebar width:_____ Grip type: _____

Front tire: _____ Front tire pressure: _____

Inner tube or bib mousse: _____

Rear tire: _____ Rear tire pressure: _____

Seat cover type: _____

Front brake pad brand and type: _____ Rear brake pad brand and type: _____

ENGINE

Fuel type:_____ Premix oil brand and ratio (if applicable):_____

Main jet:_____ Needle jet:_____ Pilot jet:_____

Clip position (from top):_____ Air screw (turns out):_____

Air filter brand:_____ Air filter oil brand:_____

Gear oil type:_____

MISCELLANEOUS

List of special accessories (i.e., handguards, skid plate, etc.):

Comments on how the bike worked (things you liked and disliked):

Chapter 3

TERRAIN AND CONDITIONS
A Sampling of What Mother Nature Has To Offer

Throughout your journeys it's very likely that you will encounter lots of different types of terrain: sand, shale, rock, mud, grass, water, hardpack, loam, water crossings, tree roots, and so on, plus all of these at various angles and speeds, and during all sorts of weather conditions. When you combine temperature, moisture, snow, wind, humidity, and whatever else Mother Nature can throw at you, there are literally a countless number of obstacles that you will encounter.

As a general rule, never go faster than feels comfortable, especially in unfamiliar terrain. While motocross and Supercross have their own brutally tough man-made obstacles, Mother Nature is full of natural booby traps that will punish you for riding beyond your limits. Therefore, it's critical that you have plenty of room to stop in case you approach something that could cause you harm.

Whenever you ride in a new area, be extremely careful. Cruise around the area at a moderate pace until you feel comfortable reading the terrain. Here's a good idea of what you will encounter:

Baked mud makes for interesting designs, but it can be extremely dangerous. While it will usually break apart with moderate pressure, sometimes it will withstand the weight of a bike and will actually become unstable and shift around.

Baked Mud

When certain types of mud dry out in the sun, they get a cracked crust on top. Although baked mud usually breaks apart easily and yields mediocre traction, sometimes it can be quite slippery, especially under braking or while turning. It all depends on the thickness of the dried layer of top soil. If it is really thick, the top layer may slide around on top of the solid soil beneath its surface. Treat it with caution.

Barbed Wire

Anywhere barbed wire is present there is a threat to man and machine. Barbed wire can cause flat tires, get entangled in your bike, or rip you off the seat. Though it is extremely difficult to see, you should use common sense and pay attention to any signs that may clue you in to its use. Look for scraps left on the ground and pay attention when you are riding near farms or other property that is sectioned off. A row of fence posts is also a clue that barbed wire is not far off.

Bushes

Though most bushes are harmless, you have to be careful. Bushes are great hiding places for football-size rocks and holes. Some bushes are strong enough to rip you off your bike if you try to punch through them.

The variations in terrain are what make riding such an incredible experience. One of the most enjoyable aspects is searching for new obstacles to conquer.

Riding over downed trees can be difficult, but it often poses an extremely fun challenge. This is National Enduro Champion Scott Plessinger wheeling over a double tree trunk in Illinois.

Cactus

When your arm looks like it was run through a cheese grater, you'll know you hit a cactus. Unlike what you see in movies, cactus doesn't always look menacing. Actually, many cactus look absolutely harmless while in bloom. If you plan to ride in a desert-type area, find out what the cactus of the area looks like before you get stung.

Downhills

Even when you are prepared, downhills can be extremely tough to tackle. Braking is tricky and the pucker factor of dropping off a 70-foot cliff wall tends to break your concentration. This effect can be amplified when downhills become an accidental excursion. If you are riding around elevation changes, be extremely alert!

Drop-Offs

This obstacle usually catches people off guard because they are not paying close enough attention to the terrain. If you cannot see the ground off in the distance, don't assume that it's all there. Instead, slow down to a safe speed and approach with caution.

Dust

If it's dusty, don't ride blind. Slow down or come to a complete stop somewhere off the racing line (sitting still in the midst of dusty track is a good way to get T-boned). If you are racing, you may consider straying off the main line (if it's safe), because many times the dust coming from another rider's bike will be isolated into a narrow band.

Fog

Treat fog like dust. Slow to a speed that you feel is safe or come to a complete stop if necessary. Fog can reduce visibility to zero, making it one of the most dangerous riding conditions imaginable.

Grass

When dry, grass provides loads of traction; however, when it's wet, grass can be extremely slippery. When you're on wet grass, treat it like ice. Stay loose, initiate turns gradually, and be ready for either wheel to slide. Early riders beware: Morning dew wets the grass considerably.

Gravel

Watch out for gravel, because riding over it is like riding over marbles. Though it may seem harmless, don't underestimate its capabilities of ripping you off your bike and pummeling you into the ground. Again, stay loose and initiate turns a little more carefully. Also note that roosting in gravel is a good way to tear the corners of your fresh rear knobby.

Hardpack

This surface usually offers very little traction, which makes acceleration, braking, and turning slightly more difficult than normal. Though there is nothing special that you have to watch out for, always remember that you can always get hurt, no matter what you are doing or how safe conditions appear. Here is

Always keep an eye out for barbed wire. It's nearly invisible, even at low speeds, and is a favorite of farmers, ranchers, and regular homeowners for marking boundaries.

a place where tires can make a huge difference. Hardpack tires have larger cornering knobs and a compound that will allow you to ride with more confidence and traction.

Ice

Pay close attention when ice is present because, if you come in contact with it, you will most likely end up on the ground. In addition to avoiding the type of ice that forms in a puddle of standing water, be aware that frozen soil also has almost zero traction. In cooler temperatures, the ground freezes and becomes a near-tractionless and rock-hard surface.

Using Trelleborg ice tires or studding your own tires can give you surprisingly good traction on ice, although they will still slide around a bit on frozen ground.

Jumps

Catching air can be a blast, but always make sure that you know what the landing area is like beforehand. Off-road jumps can be especially treacherous; for all you know you could be jumping off a cliff or into a giant bed of rock boulders.

Live Animals

Any time that you are around live animals, you have to pay close attention. Animals are very unpredictable and always pose a threat.

Loam

Moist, slightly soft soil, otherwise known as loam, is one of the finest substances known to dirt bike riders. Traction is good and the bike will rail through the corners and rocket out of the corners in a per-

fect drive. This near-perfect condition can lead to overconfidence, so be careful (but have fun).

Logs

Logs across the trail are a time-honored obstacle, one that your ancestors were endoing over long before you were a lecherous thought in your parents' minds. Techniques for crossing logs are found in the off-road section of this book. If the log looks like too much for your skills, stop and drag the bike over.

Mine Shafts

In certain parts of the country, mining once provided a prosperous way of life; how-

ever, many mine shafts are now abandoned. If you are riding in an area known to be rich in gold or other minerals, look out for open mines. A good indication is a large mound of soil that has been dug up in the middle of nowhere.

Mud

There is nothing messier than mud, and its ability to trap riders is incredible. Mud robs momentum and ruins equipment. Mud gloms on your bike in thick sheets and weighs it down. It ruins sprockets, chains, and brakes. When riding mud, stiffen your suspension a bit and gear down a tooth or two. Ride a bit more conservatively, as well.

Mud is by far the messiest type of terrain you will encounter and therefore requires extra-special attention. In addition to the goggle-prep tips you learned about in the riding gear chapter, there are several things that you should do to your bike so that it can survive. The ignition cover should be sealed to keep moisture out, and handguards should be employed to keep grips dry.

Rain

Moisture creates all sort of problems, but usually its vision-ruining capabilities are what upset off-road motorcyclists the most. Also pay attention because rain turns soil into mud rather quickly and it can be extremely slippery.

Rain Ruts

Be alert for rain ruts at all times because they are always a hazard. If you get a wheel in one, it may be difficult to get it back out safely. If you do have to cross a rain rut, do so as perpendicularly as possible and try to wheelie over them if conditions permit. This will help make sure that the front wheel doesn't get stuck within their depths or foul up your steering.

Roadkill

Treat dead animals lying on the trail like giant boulders. If you hit one, it could throw you over the handlebar or cause you to lose control of the steering. If you can't avoid one, get your weight back a bit and get on the throttle to lighten the front end.

Many top riders will use extremely porous foam to fill all crevices where mud can accumulate. The idea is to keep mud from adhering to your bike so that it doesn't add weight to it. According to Scott Summer's mechanic Fred Bramblett, mud can add more than 40 pounds to a bike unless you take the right precautions.

Right: Vines are notorious for ripping riders off their bikes. Most of the time vines are difficult to see because they are most common in shaded areas. Watch out for vines hanging from trees and those that cover the ground.

The abrasive nature of mud will eat brake pads at an astounding rate. The most common way to combat this problem is to use solid brake rotors. Eliminating the standard holes used for cooling also does away with the most common way for mud to enter the brake caliper.

TERRAIN AND CONDITIONS

- **Never ride faster than feels comfortable and safe.**
- **Always look ahead for upcoming obstacles and signs of danger.**
- **Always make sure that you are traveling at a safe speed so that you have plenty of room to apply the brakes in case you misread the terrain.**
- **Obstacles are more than rocks, jumps, trees, cactus, water, and so on. They also include other riders, cars, animals (both alive and dead), barbed wire, angry land owners, and anything else that could cause you harm.**

Snow

Though it may appear harmless, a blanket of snow can hide many dangerous obstacles such as rocks, tree roots, logs, and branches. Also, be careful when riding in snow because it makes steering, accelerating, and braking very difficult, especially when it's more than a half-foot thick. Also note that there may be ice underneath.

Trees

When riding around trees, the object is to avoid contact, for obvious reasons. Remember that most trees are immovable objects.

Tree Roots

The hard nature of tree roots makes them a particularly difficult obstacle to conquer, especially if they are hidden. When riding around trees, keep an eye out for exposed

Rocks

The sheer density of rocks make them something that you should strive to avoid. It should be rather obvious that if you hit one it can and will cause great harm to man and machine. If you have to ride over a rock bed, stay alert and watch out for jagged edges that could puncture a tire.

Sand

The nature of sand makes it tough to build and maintain momentum; therefore, it has to be treated with respect. Try to stay away from deep sand whenever possible because you may get stuck, plus it tends to overheat most engines.

Perhaps the most important motorcycle setup tip is to make sure that the airbox is effectively sealed. If water gets into your engine, it will create all sorts of problems.

roots because they will wreak havoc with steering and overall control.

Uphills

While most uphills pose little threat, watch out for variations in terrain that could produce a problem, especially in loose terrain. Take sand, for instance. If you have the throttle pinned and are producing a lot of wheelspin and suddenly come upon a rock outcropping, you could be in serious trouble once the rear wheel gets traction.

Vines

Whether or not you encounter vines depends on the part of the country in which you ride. Regardless, vines can be tough to negotiate since they want to rip you off your bike by your feet, hands, neck, and whatever else they can grab on to. While some vines break apart rather easily, others are quite strong (like steel cable) and will punish you if they are not taken seriously.

Water Crossings

When it is necessary to cross over water, look for the area that appears the shallowest and narrowest. As a rule of thumb, it's suggested that you not cross any body of water unless you can see the bottom and/or see someone else do it, plus feel totally confident making an attempt. Also remember that water can be extremely harmful to your bike, especially if it gets sucked into your intake tract. See the section on water crossings in the off-road segment of this book for more information.

Wind

There is never a time when dust is a welcome sight to motocross and off-road riders. The nature of wind makes it extremely difficult to control a motorcycle because you will find that you are always trying to overcompensate, especially in severe gusts. Though you can't avoid wind, most of the time you will have to reduce speeds or risk getting taken out by something you cannot see.

Chapter 4

BODY POSITION
The Starting Point

There are many things that will make you a better rider but none more important than developing a good understanding of basic riding position. This will lay the groundwork for all riding techniques and will eventually lead to your habits, both good and bad.

For starters, you need to develop the correct body position and make it become natural. With practice and discipline, your body will automatically slip into the correct position. The more of a habit the correct body position becomes, the better your riding will be. It's that simple.

A rider's body position is always changing with the terrain, conditions, and speed. By learning to move your body properly, you will find it easier to go fast and will use energy more efficiently. Amateur riders typically marvel at how long more advanced riders can race. Part of this comes from conditioning, but proper body position and efficient energy use are the reason top riders can finish a rugged 20-minute moto or a grueling six-hour off-road race fresher than an amateur in a 5-minute moto or one-hour enduro.

Ever notice how the winning rider often has more energy left than those behind him? Jeremy McGrath is the classic example of this and is one of the most relaxed and natural riders the sport has ever seen. A key to Jeremy's speed is his body positioning, which is flawless. When you're in the right place on the bike, everything else comes so much easier.

The basic body position is similar for off-road riders, as Ty Davis demonstrates. Your knees should be directly above the footpeg, with your weight carried on the pegs and your upper body relaxed. Note how Ty carries his weight naturally and appears relaxed and comfortable while holding good body position.

Elements of the basic body positioning include centering your weight on the seat, placing both feet on the footpegs so you can make contact with the shift lever and brake pedal, placing both hands on the controls with one or two fingers on the clutch and brake levers, positioning your elbows up, and overgripping the throttle. Gary Semics calls this the central location.

The central location puts you at the center of the motorcycle and leaves you ready for whatever comes. By raising your elbows high, your arms have some built-in flex and the proper leverage for cornering. Modern off-road bikes deliver power explosively and are capable of incredible acceleration. High elbows and a forward position help you cope with that blast of speed when you open it up.

Most often, you will be standing in the central location. Your knees should be bent slightly; they serve as additional suspension for your weight. Most of your weight should be held in your legs, with your knees gripping

Jeremy McGrath is in the attack position as he tackles this kicker jump leading into a left-hand corner. The attack position is the basic body position for most riding techniques. It starts with body weight centered, back arched slightly forward, knees bent, both feet on the pegs, elbows up, and eyes looking ahead.

Good body position is no different when airborne. Here, Steve Lamson is in perfect position, with his elbows high and head over the handlebars. Note that he has one finger on the clutch and his right wrist high enough to easily open the throttle. Mastery of off-road riding requires learning to use all of the controls smoothly, sometimes several at once.

BODY POSITIONING

- **Your head should be above the handlebar mounts (most of the time).**
- **Your knees should be bent, carrying your weight.**
- **Keep your elbows high.**
- **Overgrip the throttle.**
- **Use one or two fingers on the clutch and front brake levers.**
- **Keep your head up and look ahead at upcoming obstacles.**

the motorcycle. Your shoulders should be square and your upper body should be relaxed and supple.

Another key to the central location is that it allows you to make easy transitions on the bike. By leaning forward or back, you can add weight to the front or rear of the bike.

The central location is widely utilized because it can be effectively used in most instances with few modifications. Perhaps the central location is also preferred because it allows a rider's body to respond to shock rather quickly (as quick as your reflexes will allow), by enabling the knees, elbows, back, ankles, and wrists to absorb some of the shock. These same shock-absorbing characteristics are extremely limited when a rider is sitting.

To improve your body position, start by putting the bike on the stand and carefully going through each of Gary Semics' techniques in this chapter. He is very thorough on body position, and describes exactly where you should be on the bike.

Once you are confident that you have your body position correct, adjust your handlebars and control levers to suit. The more you change your body position, the more you will have to fiddle with ergonomics to get the bike fit.

Next, go out for a casual ride and focus on nothing but body position. Have a buddy watch you. Clue them in on what to look for, and ask for their feedback. Better yet, make a videotape of yourself riding. You'll immediately see the areas where you need work (and unless you're Jeremy McGrath, you need work).

Body positioning is the most basic skill to off-road riding. The concepts are reasonably simple, but mastering the techniques takes years of practice. Keep refining your body position, and you will improve as a rider.

Gary Semics' Absolute Techniques
BODY POSITION

Body position is one of the most important factors in riding motocross. If your body is in the correct position, you and the motorcycle become a single unit and will flow with the track. If you are out of position, things can go south in a hurry.

The fundamental aspect of body position is the central location, meaning you are in the center of the motorcycle. To master body position, the central location has to become automatic and natural. It will put you at the center of balance, a place where you can easily and naturally adjust your body to rapidly changing terrain.

Maintaining the center of balance deals with body positions and movements. This means that your body positions and movements are always in the right place at the right time.

Mastering the use of all five controls deals with the proper control of the clutch, throttle, front brake, rear brake, and the shifter. When the feeling and precision of these controls are mixed together, the rider has the ultimate control over the motorcycle.

When using the throttle, it's usually best to use the wrist. This allows your elbow to stay up. Grab on to the bars tight enough so that you feel comfortable, but not so tight that you develop arm pump. If arm pump is a problem it probably means you're gripping way too tight.

RELATED TECHNIQUES: ALL

#1 CENTER YOUR HEAD

When in the central location, sitting or standing, position your head directly above the handlebar mounts.

This will position your body in the center of the motorcycle, right over the motorcycle's pivot point. If you move forward, you are in front of the pivot point. If you move back, you are behind the pivot point.

The center of the motorcycle is where all your body movements come from and it is the center of your range of movement. Many beginner riders sit and stand with their body position too far back. This causes their weight to be behind the pivot point, causing the

motorcycle to handle poorly. This also causes arm pump because the motorcycle is pulling hard on your arms when you accelerate. So, for the proper style make sure you're doing technique #1 correctly and work from the center of the motorcycle.

Desire: "This force, which is the best thing in you, your highest self, will never respond to any ordinary half-hearted call, or any milk-and-water endeavor. It can only be reached by your supremest call, your supremest effort . . . You must back up your ambition by your whole nature, by unbounded enthusiasm and a determination to win which knows no failure."

—Orison Swett Marden

#2 KNEE POSITION

When standing in the central location, position your knee joints directly above your ankle joints. Squeeze the seat with your knees. When you move from this position, pivot from your knees where they squeeze the seat.

When you need to move forward and back on the motorcycle while standing you should move in a rowing motion while the insides of your knees slide along the sides of the motorcycle. When you move from this position you pivot from the footpegs.

A lot of beginner riders fail to squeeze the motorcycle with their

Crouch your back to weight the front wheel. Also, briefly extend your leg in corners to catch the bike if either wheel washes out. Steve Lamson and his factory Honda demonstrate.

knees, causing them to feel loose and separated from the motorcycle. In order to do the technique correctly, push out a little with your feet on the footpegs as you pinch in with your knees. This will keep you from straining the insides of your legs. Make sure your footpegs are sharp so your feet don't slip off.

When you need to move through your range of motion on the motorcycle, let your knees slide along the sides of the motorcycle, but still hold on to it with your legs.

When you have mastered these techniques you will notice more control, better endurance, and more of a connection to your iron horse.

"Everything has a price. Whatever we want in life, we must give up something to get it. The greater the value, the greater the sacrifice required. There is a high price to pay

for success. But we must realize that the rewards of true success are well worth the effort. The highway to success is a toll road."

#3 SITTING WEIGHT TRANSFER

When sitting, shift your weight by leaning your upper body rather than sliding on the seat.

Inexperienced riders often slide their butt back and forth on the seat to transfer weight. This is not correct (unless it's an exception where you have to move far).

The right way is to stay seated in the front part of the seat and lean your upper body back and forth. This simple technique will transfer more weight to the rear or front of the motorcycle and allow your body position to remain in the center of the motorcycle. This not

only gives you better control, but it's also much easier physically.

"Do not fear the winds of adversity. Remember, a kite rises against the wind rather than with it."

#4 GO WITH THE FLOW

Relax your upper body enough to flow with the motorcycle.

Most inexperienced riders and even some experienced riders get this important technique wrong, especially when they are nervous. A common mistake is to carry tension in the upper body, mostly the arms and shoulders. This causes you and the motorcycle to be top heavy, because the rider will support his weight on the handlebars. Your body will also be in the wrong position, because you cannot flow with the motorcycle if you're tense and supporting your weight on the handlebars.

Here, Jeremy McGrath is showing good form off a jump. He is forward from the attack position, with his elbows in, and head well over the front of the handlebar. Note that his foot is positioned over the brake pedal, ready to stab it when needed.

The correct way to do it is to support your weight with your legs (on the footpegs) while your upper body is relaxed enough to flow with the motorcycle. This way, you can easily change body position and can be in the right place at the right time. Carrying your weight with your legs also lowers the center of gravity so you and the motorcycle handle better.

The keys to riding motocross are balance, timing, and anticipating what is happening just before it happens. It's not in trying to force or hold things.

Remember that the first thing you need to relax is your mind. Be relaxed, clear, and ready for whatever comes up. Go with the flow.

"Obstacles are those frightful things you see when you take your mind off your goals."

#5 LOWER YOUR CENTER OF GRAVITY

Carry most of your weight on the footpegs to lower your center of gravity.

Carry your body weight on the footpegs first, the seat second, and the handlebars third. This maintains a low center of gravity in the center of the motorcycle. This technique is similar to technique #4 but the focus is on the motorcycle instead of your body.

When you are riding with a tense upper body, you are more likely to support your weight on the handlebars. This is the highest possible center of gravity the motorcycle has, and it is not a pivot point.

When the upper body is more relaxed, your body weight is carried on the footpegs. This lowers the motorcycle's center of gravity on the motorcycle at the pivot point. When you can't support your weight on the footpegs (because the inside foot is out for a corner), support your weight on the seat and the outside footpeg. These are still pivot points and they are in the center of the motorcycle.

Ride with a low center of gravity and use your legs to support your weight.

"The losers see the difficulty in every opportunity. The winners, the opportunity in every difficulty."

#6 ELBOWS UP

Keep your elbows up and out, away from your sides, while over-gripping the throttle.

A rider is giving up a lot of control if he grabs the grips straight on and rides with his forearms parallel to the ground. By doing this, he doesn't have the correct leverage factors between his upper body and the motorcycle. It's also more difficult to open the throttle.

High overgrip and high elbows will enable the rider to use the full range of the throttle in all body positions. This technique also gives you the correct leverage factors between your body and the motorcycle through your full range of movement.

Get used to this technique gradually in a safe riding area. The throttle will feel a lot different with high overgrip and it may be difficult to shut it back off once you have that sucker wide open. You don't want to leave any chili in your shorts or anything, but don't be a squid. Get those elbows up.

"Be ready when opportunity comes . . . Luck is the time when preparation and opportunity meet."

#7 SQUARE SHOULDERS

Use side-to-side movement for control. Your shoulders should stay level as you move from side to side on the motorcycle. Do not twist your upper body. Keep your shoulders centered toward the direction that you want to go.

You'll have more of a tendency to twist your upper body if you're riding with low elbows. The bad habit of twisting your upper body takes your body position out of the center of balance.

The correct way is to keep your upper body centered toward the direction that you want to go. Then move your body from side to side in order to maintain balance and make the front wheel go exactly where you want it to go. If your elbows are high you have better leverage and this is much easier to do.

Remember that the fundamentals of motocross are balance, timing, and control. Your body has to work from the correct framework in order to develop this control. Through repetition, the position has to be ingrained into your nervous system until it becomes a reflex reaction.

"**You cannot discover new oceans unless you have the courage to lose sight of the shore.**"

#8 MOVE AROUND

In general, lean forward to accelerate and back when you brake.

When you fail to do this technique correctly you end up with your body weight in the wrong place at the wrong time. This can cause you to be out of control and make you work a lot harder than you need to.

Most of the time, when you accelerate you need to lean forward into the force of acceleration and when you brake you need to lean back against the force of braking. By moving your body, you maintain the center of balance. The motorcycle and you become one operating unit and you can better maintain control.

Don't be a statue. Get used to moving on that motorcycle.

"**Teamwork is the ability to work together toward a common vision, the ability to direct individual accomplishment toward organizational objectives. It is the fuel that allows common people to attain uncommon results.**"

#9 BACK POSITION

Straighten your back when leaning forward; crouch your back when moving back.

Riders commonly keep their backs in one position (always crouched or always straight). This is a bad habit because it is more physically demanding. Back position should change according to body position on the motorcycle.

When you're in the forward body position, your back should be straight. This allows you to get up and over the front of the motorcycle. When you're in the back body position, your back should be crouched. This will allow you to lower your center of gravity and give you better control.

These are definitely good techniques to frequently practice in a stationary position before you try it on the track. Remember, there's more suspension on the motorcycle than the forks and shock. Use all of your body, including your back.

"**Success is a journey, not a destination.**"

#10 FOOT POSITION

Ride with the balls of your feet on the footpegs.

Some riders never ride with the balls of their feet on the footpegs. To see what category you fall into, check the wear marks on the bottom of your boots. If you are one of these riders you are missing out on the extra control you could be having from riding with the balls of your feet on the footpegs.

A general rule to go by is that if you're not using the shifter or brake, you should be on the balls of your feet. When you need to use the shifter or brake, simply move up to the arches of your feet, then move back to the balls of your feet when you're done braking or shifting. While riding, you are frequently changing back and forth. This is true whether sitting or standing.

The benefits to riding on the balls of your feet are: it adds another joint to your body's suspension (your ankle joint) for better movement and feel, your feet won't hit the ground in ruts and get ripped off the footpegs, and you won't hit the shifter or brake by accident.

This is definitely one of those techniques that you have to think about and practice separately. Keep checking the bottom of those boots.

"**Develop success from failures. Discouragement and failure are two of the surest stepping stones to success. No other element can do so much for a man if he is willing to study and make capital out of them.**"
—*Dale Carnegie*

#11 FOOT POSITION WHILE BRAKING

When using the shifter or brake, the arch of your foot should be on the footpeg.

This is so you can reach the shifter and brake and operate them correctly with the right leverage factors. Sometimes a rider might get it wrong and his own feet will actually get in the way. This can happen when you have the arches of your feet on the footpegs and you are not using the shifter or brake. What can get you into trouble is that you may hit the shifter or brake by mistake, which can knock the tranny into a false neutral (between gears) or throw you forward if you hit the rear brake unexpectedly. Either of these things could be minor mishaps or major traumas, depending on when they occur.

To avoid this, tilt your toes out away from the shifter and brake when you want to remain on the arches of your feet, but you do not want to use the shifter or brake. This is especially useful when you have too short of a time between shifting and braking to move from your arches to the balls of your feet.

With practice and experience, you'll know just how far you need to tilt your toes out and you'll notice if you happen to bump the shifter or brake by accident.

Feeling, timing, anticipation, and coordination in motocross add up to total flow concentration. This is one of the most rewarding sensations you can find. There may be many things that come close, but none of them can beat total flow concentration.

"When your desires are strong enough, you will appear to possess superhuman powers to achieve."

—Napoleon Hill

Most riders always keep at least one finger on the clutch at all times. Depending on the difficulty of clutch pull and your own personal style, you may end up using two fingers, but you will have a better grip on the bars if you can train yourself to use one. The same goes for the front brake.

#12 FOOT POSITION WHILE SHIFTING

When you're accelerating and your body position is in the forward position, lift your foot off the footpeg in order to shift.

Most entry-level riders make the mistake of sliding their butt back on the seat in order to shift. This is so they can keep their foot on the footpeg and use the footpeg as a pivot point to lift the front of their foot up to shift. They are compromising their body position in order to shift.

When you're upshifting, your body position is usually forward because you are accelerating. This means that in order to upshift you have to lift your foot up off the footpeg. This means you are using your whole leg to shift.

Remember to keep that shift lever adjusted so it's level with the top of the footpeg. If you adjust it too low, you're going to have a hard time reaching it to downshift, getting your foot under it to upshift, and run the risk of the engine being knocked out of gear in a rut.

A good way to practice your shifting is when you're working on your starts.

"Every great man has become great, every successful man has succeeded, in proportion as he has confined his powers to one particular channel."

#13 ONE OR TWO FINGERS ON THE CLUTCH

Use one or two fingers on the clutch and keep those fingers on the clutch at all times.

This is an important technique, and it takes a lot of practice to master. The most common mistake here is to hold onto the grip with all four fingers and then grab the clutch with all four fingers. This makes using the clutch awkward and, as a result, riders don't use the clutch often enough.

A pro rider has one or two fingers on the clutch lever 99 percent of the time. He uses it out of corners, through whoops, jumps, and certain kinds of bumps to help deliver the exact amount of power to the rear wheel how and when he wants it.

The clutch should be used almost every time the throttle goes from closed to open, so if you want good, controlled power, learn to use that low end lever.

"Bring all your mind and faculties to bear without distraction on the problem or subject at hand."

#14 HAND DEXTERITY

Learn to work the levers and hold on to the grips independently.

The most common mistake riders make is holding on to the grips with all four fingers and then grabbing at the levers only when they really have to use them. This is so awkward that riders don't use the clutch and front brake levers often enough and when they do use the levers, they can't hold on to the grips well.

It takes time and practice to develop the ability to hold on to the grips and work the levers accurately at the same time. Many riders use two fingers on the clutch, many use one finger. It's best to use one finger on the front brake. Get used to it and make it a habit.

Give up a finger or two on the grips in order to work the levers independently from holding onto the grips.

Success: "The ability to apply your physical and mental energies to one problem incessantly without growing weary."

—Thomas A. Edison

Chapter 5

The Fine Art of Slowing Down

BRAKING

Braking may seem like one of the easiest tasks in the dynamic world of motorcycle riding, but in reality, it's one of the most difficult techniques to perfect. Brake power, rider style, terrain, and line choice all factor in to the equation. It's not as simple as grabbing a handful of front brake and standing on the rear brake pedal, but there are some general rules that work in most situations. Also note that the brakes can be used for more than just slowing down. The brakes can help you hold a line in a turn. Tapping the rear brake while in the air will drop the front wheel, as well.

Most of the stopping power of the brakes comes from the front brake. When braking, the weight of the bike will naturally transfer to the front wheel. With the rear wheel "light" (barely skimming the ground), the traction is all in the front wheel, and stopping power is in the front brakes. A bit of rear brake helps keep the bike straight and provides a bit of additional stopping power, but when you want to haul the bike down from warp nine to zero, the lever on the right side of the bars is where you'll find the most help.

Body Position

Body positioning is the most critical element of effective braking, and for many reasons. In general, most braking is done in the standing position with most rider weight to-

There are several products designed to provide more powerful braking, and serious riders and racers will experiment with the new technology. Items like softer brake pads and 10- to 30-mm oversized rotors can increase stopping power dramatically.

ward the back of the bike, near the end of the seat or the front of the rear fender. This additional weight on the rear end will help keep the back end of the bike on the ground and provide better control. The rearward positioning of the rider will also provide more leverage through the arms and legs to keep the back

end of the bike from coming around and swapping.

The key here is to keep adjusting to terrain and conditions. There is no one set point for braking; you need to make subtle adjustments to keep the bike stable, with both wheels at least touching the ground.

Ricky Carmichael's body position allows him to set up for the next obstacle. This sitting technique is usually difficult to achieve because of terrain conditions, but here Ricky has found a smooth patch of real estate to execute this move. Notice that he's not using the front brake; instead, he has chosen to steer with the throttle and control his speed with only the brake pedal.

"I find myself constantly moving my weight back and forth on the bike to achieve the desired body positioning while braking," claims multi-time AMA Supercross Champion Jeremy McGrath. "A couple inches either way makes a big difference."

Brake Straight

Most of your braking to slow the bike will take place in a straight line. When the bike is turning, heavy braking will make the tires slide, or push, through the turns. This is what you want when brake-sliding the rear, but a front-wheel slide is harder to recover from. When a rider uses the front brake too aggressively in a turn, the front wheel is prone to tucking under, which usually results in a low-side crash.

The most effective way to reduce the pushing effect is to apply less power to the front brake and/or steer with the throttle—that is, use the power of the motor to help you turn. This may seem like an odd technique, especially in a chapter devoted to braking, but in some turns, like chicanes, the bike may handle better because the effects of braking and applying the throttle will upset the suspension less.

The other common scenario that happens when turning and braking at the same time occurs when the back end of the motorcycle can't slow down at the same rate as the front. In essence, the extra momentum carried by the rear end makes the back want to come around somewhat perpendicular to the track. In extreme cases, the bike can actually do a 180-degree spin. This is desirable for a brake-slide, but can surprise a rider when the back end squirts out unexpectedly. If you are caught off-guard, the back end can come around, catch, and pitch you off in a high-side crash.

Back to braking a straight line, though. From a technical standpoint, the back end shouldn't come around on one side if the bike is in a perfectly straight line. Stated as simply as possible, the mass of the rear end would instead push the steering stem against the steering head, which in turn would put more weight on the front of the motorcycle. This is precisely why a bike will endo (while braking in a straight line) when body positioning is incorrect or in instances of overbraking. Once again, this is the result of the rear wheel not being able to slow down the back end of the bike at the same rate as the front.

Braking Bumps Part 1

1. These two sequences clearly show the effect that braking bumps have on body positioning and suspension. Each sequence was shot in the same race to create the most realistic comparison. This particular corner has two small bumps that most riders couldn't double. As Greg Albertyn enters the section, he's standing in the attack position, but is hard on the brakes as evidenced by the puff of dirt flying up from the rear wheel.

2. This extremely aggressive approach requires Albee to shift his weight to the back of the bike. Experience has taught him that the back end will kick up as he rapidly decelerates and slams into the initial bump at race speed. Note that he is using both brakes simultaneously, but is very cautious about using too much front brake because it increases the likelihood of an endo due to a prediction of the rear-wheel hop you'll see in the next few photos.

3. As expected, Albertyn got a big hop from the effects of his suspension reacting to the first bump under braking. This hop is partially due to the position of his fork and shock in the suspension stroke. Upon braking, the resistance has caused both ends to collapse somewhat, which has positioned the suspension in a stiffer part of the stroke. To combat this "problem," Albertyn has readjusted his weight, placed his butt over the rear fender, and stretched out his arms to simultaneously push the front end down.

4. Proper planning has allowed Albee to maintain control and enter the corner in the line he has chosen. Maintaining full control is essential for effective braking.

BRAKING

Jeremy McGrath— "Experiment with different brake pad compounds for different types of tracks and terrain. Some brake pads are super sensitive while others aren't—it's just a matter of personal preference. Usually softer compounds make for better stopping but wear out quicker, and vice versa."

Steve Lamson— "Bleed your brakes whenever you sense a little mushiness. Powerful brakes are vital for effective stopping."

John Dowd— "We use oversize rotors (approximately 10 millimeters larger) on the front of our works bikes for more stopping power. It doesn't make that big a difference, but it is a slight advantage."

Steve Lamson— "New tires make a big difference in braking. The square edges of new knobbies provide way more traction than old tires that are rounded."

Skip Norfolk— "Always make sure that your rotors are clean. Even a hint of oil residue can ruin pads and decrease the effectiveness of your brakes. If there is any doubt, clean your rotors with brake cleaner."

Danny Carlson— "I always adjust my brake lever and pedal so there is virtually no play. I like my brakes really touchy. It doesn't work for all people, but it works for me."

Though you may not like to hear that the front end of your bike can push at all speeds, or worse, endo, these problems can be reduced through proper braking. In most cases, both brakes should be applied evenly and in a progressive manner, and you should begin braking early enough so that you have time to momentarily back off the brakes in case overbraking fouls up the handling.

Most of the time brakes are used together. Using only the rear brake is useful for brake-sliding. The front is best used with a bit of rear brake, which helps keep the bike straight and provides a bit more stopping power.

Brake-Slides

Brake-slides are good ways to turn very quickly, although they rob momentum. They work better in flat turns, but good riders learn to do them on most any camber. The principle is no different than the one you probably used to slide your bicycle around. Pull in the clutch, lock the rear brake, and gently turn the motorcycle right or left. The rear will shoot out, and the back end will swing around. The key to making a brake-slide useful is to coordinate the brake and throttle so that you go in doing a brake-slide and come out in a controlled power slide. This takes a lot of practice, and riders should start cautiously. Work in an open, flat area if possible, and try it at low speeds. Once you get it down, it is a great way to pass someone on the inside.

When using the rear brakes, most of the time it will be necessary to pull in the clutch to make sure your engine doesn't stall if the rear wheel locks up, especially at slower speeds. For the same reason, you may have to rev your engine while braking if your bike doesn't idle.

One of the most important aspects is to remember that brakes are only effective when the wheels are touching the ground. You also want to avoid landing off jumps with the brakes applied because this will dramatically change the way the bike will handle. The suspension usually won't respond well, plus it increases the odds of the tires sliding out.

Elevation Braking

Braking technique changes when riding on slopes. When traveling downhill, you have to adjust your body position to keep some weight on the rear wheel. Aggressive use of the front

5. Since Albertyn has maintained the attack position he's able to "blip" the throttle as the rear wheel comes in contact with the second bump, and actually avoids a small hole that has been created on the other side. This allows the suspension to settle, and now Albee's in good position to execute a turn.

Braking Bumps Part 2

1. Doug Henry has found a creative line around the same obstacle. This is one of the rewards of riding the edges of the track and continuing to look at the changing lines. Here he rides around the outside of the jump and doesn't upset his suspension.

brake on a downhill will weight the front end to a larger degree than on level parts of the track. This can be compensated for by moving your body back a bit farther, but it is a problem when the terrain is rough. If you are braking aggressively, the front suspension will be loaded with most of the rider's and the bike's weight. If you hit a big braking bump, the suspension will probably bottom and the bike may endo, pitching the rider over the bars. To avoid this,

plan your braking carefully on a downhill so that you can release or brake lightly over braking bumps or similar obstacles.

Downhills also require earlier braking because it is much more difficult to brush off momentum. If you find that you are going too fast and don't feel comfortable applying the front brake, you can attempt to traverse the hill much like the technique that snow skiers use to slow down.

2. Because he's not worried about making major body changes, Henry's able to drive into the turn much harder than Albertyn and set up for the actual turn much sooner. At this point he's already got his foot out, ready to make the left-hand turn.

3. Henry's just about finished with braking and is making final preparations to enter the turn. A split second later he's off the brakes and back on the throttle. Also note that Henry used much less energy in this section and has maintained more control the entire time.

In contrast, braking while traveling uphill is much easier because the weight of the bike and rider is naturally carried to the rear, plus the natural forces of gravity make it extremely easy to brush off speed. For these reasons, you will probably find that you can brake much later than you normally could on level ground.

Slippery Conditions and Off-Cambers

Traction also plays an important role in deceleration. In most situations, the goal should be to look for a line that offers the most grip. When possible, avoid sand, mud, or other slick surfaces. When you have to

BRAKING

- Body position is crucial. Most braking is done in the standing position with knees bent, elbows up, and weight back a bit.
- Adjust body position to keep the rear wheel on the ground.
- Complete most of your braking before initiating the turn.
- Apply the brakes progressively.
- Avoid locking up the front wheel.
- Choose lines that avoid sand, mud, or braking bumps when possible.
- Brake before or after braking bumps.
- Apply the brakes more gently on slippery surfaces such as sand, mud, snow, ice, or other slick surfaces.

brake when traction is poor, use the brake more gently and progressively.

For this very reason you also want to avoid overly aggressive braking on off-cambers. The nature of off-cambers allows fewer tire treads to grip, and only those on one side of the tire, which will allow the front end of a bike to twist and slide out.

On slippery surfaces and off-cambers, you have to be more conservative with the brakes. Since the tires are prone to locking up easier on slippery surfaces, braking must be done with finesse and less power.

"I rarely use the front brake in deep sand," says 1995 AMA 125cc National Motocross Champion Steve Lamson. "I notice that the front wheel tends to dig in and causes the back end of the bike to swap. When I do use the front brake in sand, I apply it very slowly and don't use much force."

It is also important to analyze braking bumps very carefully. When possible, stay clear of them. Braking bumps make it extremely tough to brush off speed quickly because they make the suspension more active. Braking bumps also tend to tire riders easily and induce arm pump easier than most other obstacles. You may want to get most of your braking done before or after crossing braking bumps, so you can let off of the brakes and let the suspension work over the bumps.

Front Brake

The brakes do more than slow down the motorcycle. Used properly, they add precision to your control of the machine. Begin with proper foot and hand position and move on to these advanced techniques.

Don't forget that if you aren't braking or accelerating, you are going to get passed.

Many riders use the front brake to help them settle into corners, as shown by Jimmy Button. He is using a little front brake to make sure the front end doesn't run away from him as he negotiates this section, which is slightly off-camber.

RELATED TECHNIQUES: BODY POSITION, ACCELERATION, CORNERING

#15 REAR BRAKING WHILE STANDING

When standing, pivot the arch of your foot on the footpeg and depress the rear brake pedal with the ball of your foot.

Some riders have different parts of their foot on the footpeg when using the rear brake. Sometimes they are on the arch and sometimes they are on the heel. They fail to develop the proper habit and feeling of controlling the rear brake.

When you're standing while using the rear brake always have the footpeg in the arch of your foot, right in front of the heel. Then your foot can pivot on the footpeg and give you the same good feel of the rear brake every time. Find the control.

"You learn that, whatever you are doing in life, obstacles don't matter very much. Pain or other circumstances can be there, but if you want to do a job bad enough, you'll find a way to get it done."
—Jack Youngblood

#16 REAR BRAKING WHILE SITTING

When sitting, lift your foot off the footpeg and depress the rear brake pedal with the ball of your foot.

As you hold your braking leg up, keep that leg tight against the side of the motorcycle. As soon as you finish with the rear brake, put your foot back on the footpeg.

Most beginning riders get all mixed up either when standing or sitting while braking. This is because there is one braking technique for standing (which we just covered) and one braking technique for sitting, and they are very different.

Some riders try to keep their foot on the footpeg and use the rear brake while sitting. This won't work while sitting on the front of the seat, because your foot and ankle just won't bend that far. Some riders use their heel on the rear brake while sitting, which is not good either.

If you watch a pro, you'll see that he lifts his foot up off the footpeg, locks his leg in place against the side of the motorcycle, and uses the ball of his foot on the rear brake by flexing his ankle. This technique will give you the most control.

Practice this with the bike on the stand first, then while the bike is moving.

"The obstacles you face are mental barriers which can be broken by adopting a more positive approach."

#17 REAR BRAKING DURING TRANSITION

To control the rear brake through the transition from standing to sitting, lift your right foot as you sit and shift your weight to the left footpeg.

Wouldn't it be terrible if every time you went from standing to sitting you had to let go of the rear brake or you couldn't control the rear brake anymore? Just because you're going from standing to sitting doesn't mean you don't need the rear brake. In fact, that just might happen to be the place where you need it the most.

We just covered how to use the rear brake while standing and while sitting. There must also be control between standing and sitting. As you begin to sit down for the corner, lift your right foot off the footpeg and still control the rear brake. This means your weight has to shift to the left footpeg until you get your weight to the front part of the seat. Then, as you're sitting on the front part of the seat, lock your leg against the side of the motorcycle, and hold your leg above the rear brake as you use it with the ball of your foot.

Practice this with the bike on the stand at first, then while the bike is moving.

"Courage is a special kind of knowledge. It is knowledge of how to fear what ought to be feared and how not to fear what ought not to be feared."

Small Braking Bumps

1. Greg Albertyn approaches this section once again in the attack position and can be more aggressive than in his previous sequence.

2. Albee's once again experiencing some rear wheel hop, but this time it's less noticeable. Again, he repositions his body weight, places his butt over the rear fender, and extends his arms to push the front end down. Notice how much abuse the fork takes under these circumstances.

3. At this point another interesting situation occurs. The line leading into the corner starts to bend and Albertyn is forced to back off slightly on the front brake.

4. Albertyn almost throws it away here. He's been overly aggressive with the front end and his tire has started to plow (notice the roost coming off the front wheel). At this point he lets go of the front brake and tries to stand the bike straight up to avoid crashing.

#18 CLUTCH OUT WHILE BRAKING

When braking into a corner, downshift and leave the clutch out. Let the back pressure of the engine help slow you down. This is like an anti-lock system. While braking, only pull the clutch in when you want to lock up the rear wheel.

The wrong techniques in braking will cause you to lose time and could even get you into trouble. When a rider comes into a corner carrying too much speed for his ability to slow down for the corner you'll see him doing all kinds of panic braking—from locking up the rear wheel at 40 miles per hour to free wheeling, and back to sliding again.

The proper way is good, steady, controlled braking. You should start off with hard braking and then progressively lighter and lighter braking as you enter the corner. This proper technique works far better if you leave the clutch out as you brake and downshift for the corner (don't use the clutch to downshift). This way the engine will help to slow you down and cause a more steady braking effect. The rear wheel has the best braking effect just before it locks up.

If you can't do this technique well, you need to practice your control of the rear brake lever.

"Do not pray for tasks equal to your powers. Pray for powers equal to your tasks."

#19 DOWNSHIFT WITH-OUT THE CLUTCH

You do not need to use the clutch when you downshift.

Some inexperienced riders use the clutch to downshift and then just hold it in while they brake the rest of the way into the corner. Using the clutch to downshift is not necessary. By leaving the clutch out while braking, the engine's back pressure will make your braking smooth and steady.

It is necessary to use the clutch when you upshift because the transmission has torque on the gears from the power of the engine. But there is very little torque on the gears when the throttle is off and you're slowing down. So leave that low-end lever (the clutch) out when you're downshifting and braking for a corner.

"Confidence doesn't come from nowhere. It's a result of something; hours and days and weeks and years of constant work and dedication."

—Roger Staubach

#20 DRAG THE REAR BRAKE OVER OBSTACLES

Dragging the rear brake will reduce the tendency of the rear wheel to kick up on certain bumps and obstacles.

When a beginner rider gets into trouble, like having the rear wheel kick up too high, he usually just freezes and waits to see what happens. One thing you can do to avoid this kicking up effect is to drag the rear brake when you think the rear wheel is going to kick up. This puts a little downforce on the rear suspension and greatly reduces the kick of the rear wheel.

The next time you see that you're going to hit a big bump or a whoop harder than you wanted to, touch or drag that rear brake and you'll see how much it holds the rear end down. I know it saved me many times from an endo.

This is another good reason you need to be able to use the rear brake from any body position on the motorcycle, because in this case, you will be standing with your weight back.

"Very few persons, comparatively, know how to Desire with sufficient intensity. They do not know what it is to feel and manifest that intense, eager, longing, craving, insistent, demanding, ravenous Desire which is akin to the drowning man for a breath of air, of the shipwrecked or desert lost man for a drink of water, of the famished man for bread and meat."

—Robert Collier

5. **Quick thinking has allowed Albee to save it. He finishes up his braking with the rear brake. Notice that he's remained in the attack position the entire time.**

Braking Seated

In low-speed corners without braking bumps, it is fairly common for riders to do all of their braking while seated. The low speed and lowered center of gravity reduce the risk of an endo. Typically both the front and rear brakes are applied evenly.

Chapter 6

ACCELERATION
More Than Just a Handful of Throttle

Acceleration is one of the most critical aspects in all of motorcycling, and the reason is simple. The harder you accelerate, the faster you go. Getting a clean drive can be the key to everything from a clean setup for a pass to clearing a big jump.

Acceleration is, however, more than just grabbing a handful of throttle and unleashing all the ponies in your stable. Accelerating correctly is a blend of proper body position, throttle control, clutch use, and line choice. Sound familiar?

Before a rider can think about line choice there has to be some type of goal with your acceleration. Most of the time, riders strive for the shortest route because it's presumably quicker, but imagine if a rider is tackling a nasty uphill or attempting a Supercross-style triple jump. In these situations it may be necessary to get a better run at the obstacle in order to increase speed and momentum; therefore, it's important to look at each situation very carefully.

"Try to maintain momentum as best as possible," insists Steve Lamson. "It's much easier to accelerate when you've already got speed. If you come to a complete stop, your bike has to work harder and you'll have a difficult time getting traction."

It's also much more efficient to accelerate in a straight line than it is while turning because your bike has less resistance and the tire has more contact surface with the ground.

Momentum

One way to get a better drive is to choose lines that allow you to carry more speed through a corner. Doug Henry and his factory Yamaha demonstrate.

Terrain also determines the difficulty of acceleration. In loam, where traction is abundant, acceleration will be relatively easy, but you will have to fight the bike's natural tendency to wheelie. In sharp contrast, it's a battle to find traction on dry hardpack or in sand (both shallow and deep). As a result, it's easy to break the rear wheel loose and lose control.

Regardless of the terrain type, the quest for traction (which leads to acceleration) involves a series of body repositionings to keep both wheels on the ground. Ideally you want to keep as much weight on the rear wheel as possible so that it will stay in constant contact with the ground, but you also need to avoid wheeling. If a bike starts to wheelie, most

A good drive out of a corner can set you up for a pass, cut down your lap times, or just feel great. The key is getting the rear wheel hooked up and keeping the bike straight. Jeremy McGrath is shown doing both in fine fashion, and weighting the front end by leaning forward.

likely it will lose speed and, if the rider is not prepared, it could cause him to chop the throttle, thus reducing your drive.

"To reduce the chances of wheelying, place your body weight over the front of the bike," instructs Steve Lamson. "One of the exceptions would be downhills where most of the time you would want to stand with your weight towards the back of the bike."

Fresh tires are also a key to a good drive. "To get the best acceleration, you must have good tires, preferably new ones, that are designed for the terrain," says Lamson. "Otherwise, you'll get too much wheelspin and it will be impossible to get the best drive."

Another foe that hinders acceleration is called acceleration bumps. These obstacles, usually found in a series and ranging up to a foot or so tall, foul up suspension and make acceleration difficult. Ideally riders in this situation should search for an alternative line that provides a smoother route, but one may not always be available. When forced to negotiate acceleration bumps, the best way is to let your knees and elbows work with the suspension to keep it on the ground as much as possible. You can also traverse these obstacles a gear higher than usual. This will lessen the torque effect of the chain and allow the rear suspension to soak up the bumps and keep the back tire on the ground. The engine won't be shrieking at peak rpm, but your drive will be stronger and smoother.

"If there are a lot of acceleration bumps you may want to try to wheelie over them," says Jeremy McGrath. "Try to get your front wheel to skim over the top of them so that your front suspension won't be affected. This will allow the shock to do its job and keep the rear wheel on the ground as much as possible."

McGrath's approach is very aggressive and requires precise throttle control to make sure the front wheel doesn't rise too quickly and cause the rider to lose control. There are, however, times where you may consider slowing down to actually speed your travel. "Sometimes, in order to accelerate the hardest you have to be patient," says Ron Lechien. "In some cases, if you get on the throttle too hard too soon, you can make mistakes that will cost you time. To prevent this, practice rolling on the throttle without using the clutch. This will also help you determine which gear works best, but it will help make you a smoother rider. And if you

Acceleration Bumps

Putting power to the ground is sometimes a difficult task, especially in uneven terrain. When acceleration bumps become too large, it's necessary to stand, as James Dobb does as he exits this turn. *Joe Bonnello*

Controlling Wheelies

This is a good example of weighting the front end to keep the bike from wheelying. Notice how Jimmy Button has his upper torso over the fuel tank and handlebar. If the front end comes up too much, slip the clutch ever so slightly to drop the front wheel without destroying the drive.

Changing Lines

1. Mike LaRocco has decided that the rut used by other riders has gotten too deep to use effectively. Instead, he's slowed his entrance speed and cut the corner sharper.

can be smooth and make few mistakes, usually you'll become faster."

Lechien also points out that gearing can make a big difference in the drive you get out of the corners. "Make sure your bike is geared correctly for your type of riding; otherwise, acceleration will be hindered," Lechien says.

Ideally, you should be able to come out of a corner and get a good drive by rolling the throttle open with perhaps a quick stab at the clutch. If you find that several corners require either excessive clutch abuse in one gear while another gear you exit and immediately overrev, try changing the final gearing. A tooth or two less on the rear sprocket is great for subtle changes, while changing the gearing on the front sprocket will provide larger changes.

ACCELERATION

• Select the proper gear that will allow the engine to work the most efficiently.
• Avoid wheelspin through careful throttle control and clutch use.
• Search for lines that offer the most traction.
• Use your legs to absorb acceleration bumps while standing.
• Try to carry as much momentum as possible.
• Adjust your weight forward and backward to find a delicate balance that will give the rear wheel traction without allowing the bike to wheelie.
• Acceleration is most effective in a straight line.

2. Since he reduced his speed more than normal to hug the inside of the turn, it's much easier for him to lose traction under hard acceleration. As you can see, he's already starting to get sideways as he drives out of the turn.

3. At this point LaRocco has become too aggressive and is forced to get out of the throttle to straighten the bike. Had he continued to stay on the gas, he probably would have slid out and his body been tossed off the highside.

Gary Semics' Absolute Techniques
ACCELERATION

As with the brakes, the throttle should be used for much more than just speeding up. A bit of power to the rear wheel can be used to place the front wheel and is key to jumping and whoops. With modern off-road motorcycles, the fundamental skill of using the throttle is modulation. Your bike is a powerful, explosive weapon. Learn to use that power precisely, like a surgeon with a scalpel.

Once again, you should be either on the gas or on the brakes. Don't coast.

Smooth Power

Getting the tire hooked up requires coordinated use of the clutch and throttle. When traction is good, you have to be careful not to use too much throttle and wheelie. When traction is poor, the trick is to get the tire hooked up at all. In most cases, smooth application of power is key. Jimmy Button is shown in fine form. Note that his body is over the handlebars, weighting the front end, and his left foot is in position, ready to shift up.

RELATED SECTIONS: BODY POSITION, WHOOPS, JUMPS, BRAKING, CORNERING

#21 USE THE CLUTCH

Whenever you accelerate hard, use the clutch and throttle together.

When accelerating hard, many beginning riders simply open the throttle and wait for the engine to build rpms to reach the meat of the powerband. Once in a while they might get lucky and just happen to be near the powerband, but if they're too far below the powerband they won't get the power they want when they need it.

Of course, you need to be in the right gear for the amount of speed and momentum you're carrying. Don't slip the clutch too much. In this case, the clutch is just a helper, not a means. When this technique is done correctly you can utilize more of the power of the engine. This is because you can begin to accelerate from the bottom of the powerband instead of starting from the middle or near the top.

By using the clutch and throttle together you cause the engine to build the right amount of rpms just how and when you want them. By slipping the clutch a little, the engine will come in on the powerband. If you just use the throttle, the engine may bog and hesitate before it can reach the powerband.

"Concentrate, put all your eggs in one basket, and watch that basket."
—Andrew Carnegie

#22 FRONT WHEEL PLACEMENT

Use the clutch and throttle as you pull up on the handlebars in order to carry the front wheel a little farther down the track and set it down where you want. This is called front wheel placement.

The common mistake here is to just let the front wheel bounce, hit, and land wherever it may, just by chance. If you do this, you're going to be in for a rough ride and you'll have to slow down to compensate for it.

Pro riders have the ability to lift, carry, and set the front wheel down

Standing Drives

To get the best drive on extremely fast areas, it may be necessary to stand up. Here Brian Swink is able to absorb some of the acceleration bumps with his knees, thus helping the suspension keep the rear wheel hooked up.

Water & Rocks

You have to be extremely careful when accelerating in stream beds. It's difficult to tell what's beneath the surface and it can often spell disaster if you get overly aggressive.

wherever they want in order to miss bumps and land in G-out troughs to smooth things out.

Of course, you need to pull back on the bars and maintain the correct body positions, but the other half is accomplished with the clutch and throttle. Use the clutch and throttle together in order to deliver just the right amount of power to the rear wheel in order to carry the front wheel to where you want to place it.

"Always bear in mind that your own resolution to succeed is more important than any other one thing."

—*Abraham Lincoln*

Chapter 7

CORNERING
A Look at the World of Turns

There are many variables that determine how fast a motorcycle can be turned: speed, available traction, terrain type, amount of turning, body positioning, and throttle control. Of those ingredients you usually have control only over the latter two; yet paired, they encompass thousands of combinations that make cornering very, very challenging.

While cornering doesn't offer the thrill of jumping, cliff climbing, or some of the airborne aspects of the sport, it is probably the most common challenge you will encounter. It is also the best place on the track to pass. For this simple reason, you should spend a fair amount of your time working on your cornering technique, especially if racing is on your agenda.

Good technique starts with body positioning that, ideally, is designed to lower your center of gravity and maintain traction at both wheels. In most cases this means sitting down, shifting your weight to the furthermost forward portion of your seat, sticking your inside leg out and applying pressure to the outside footpeg. When combined with cautious throttle application to make sure the front end doesn't come off the ground or the rear wheel slide out, this is the foundation for developing good cornering habits.

Even though you are sitting most of the time, it is important that you are still able to absorb some of the bumps with your knees and elbows. In most cases you want to stay very relaxed in the turns so that you can help

Outside Line

1. This banked turn offers a variety of lines. On the inside there is a rut, in the middle it's smooth, and on the outside there is a berm. Steve Lamson has determined that in this case the outside is the faster line. Because there was a kicker jump leading into the turn, Lamson is still in the standing position and is still finishing his braking while trying to go as straight as possible.

your suspension soak up whatever changes in the terrain are thrown your way. If you are rigid, your bike will get bounced around all over the place, and, if your wheels break contact with the ground, you increase your chances of falling down.

Jeremy McGrath is known for his textbook riding style, as this shot perfectly illustrates. Notice that his elbows are up and his body weight is forward. This is why he is one of the best riders the sport has ever produced.

2. In a split second, Lamson has shifted his body position and has begun the actual turn using the berm for traction-inducing resistance. Furthermore, Lamson's off both brakes and is leaning into the turn.

3. As Lamson reaches the apex of the turn, he gets back on the throttle, as evidenced by the roost. Notice how he keeps his inside leg out in case a wheel slips out until he has the bike aimed totally straight. Also, throughout the entire turn he weights the outside footpeg to produce better traction to both wheels.

Ready To Dab

Because it can feel awkward leaning into a turn, most riders find it natural to put out a leg in case a small dab is required. "When you stick your leg out you have got to make sure that you keep it in front of your body," says Jeremy McGrath. "It won't do you any good if it slides back because you won't have any leverage to support your weight."

"When you stick your leg out, make sure your toes are pointed up," says Ron Lechien. "This way if your boot catches on something it should deflect off the sole instead of causing your foot to get bent back."

Like all techniques, there are many variations that you will find helpful. In extremely high-speed sections you may find it necessary to stand, especially if the areas are too rough for your suspension to handle with you in the seated position. When you stand through a turn, try to weight the front of the motorcycle to make sure the front wheel has traction, but keep both feet on the footpegs. This way you can control your balance better, plus you can use both knees to absorb changes in the terrain.

Gear Selection

Regardless of whether you are sitting or standing, most riders agree that it is best, in most cases, to pick one gear and stick with it until you are out of the turn. "Usually I try not to shift in a corner," says Danny Carlson. "I make sure that my bike is in the correct gear when I enter the turn because it saves time and it's much smoother. The only time I find that I am forced to shift mid-turn is at the exit around big sweepers where my bike would normally tend to overrev. When the bike over-revs, the power falls off pretty abruptly and it slows your drive."

Another important aspect is line choice in the turn. "Try to make your arch smooth," says Jeremy McGrath. "Any quick movements will cause you to lose traction easier. That's why you also want to roll on the throttle and stay off the clutch as much as possible. It's always difficult trying to figure out just how hard you can get on the gas."

"If there is a banking around the outside you may want to use it because it will give you more traction than a flat turn," adds Lechien. "Also look for any good ruts. If you find a good rut that you can rail, you can get on the gas harder and turn quicker."

4. Though Lamson is leaning his bike over, notice how he keeps his body almost perfectly straight up and down. This helps him maintain traction.

5. The final product is a mistake-free arch as Lamson powers to the next obstacle.

Bermed (or banked) corners can be extremely helpful because they offer a lot more resistance for your tires and usually decrease the chances of losing traction. Unfortunately, most berms are located at the outermost edge of turns, which forces you to take the long route, which can actually be slower than a more risky inside line. Ultimately you have to determine which is better for you.

Ruts

In contrast, most ruts will develop at the inside of turns first. When used properly, ruts can be the express way around a turn, but they can also be hazardous. The most common problem occurs when a rider is too aggressive and carries too much momentum into a rutted turn and can't get both wheels firmly seated into the groove.

The idea with rutted turns is to line up with the rut prior to the entrance so that both wheels will drive in naturally. If one wheel doesn't line up, there's an increased chance that you will fall.

Once both wheels are in the rut, it is important that you maintain momentum. In most cases this will require moderate throttle application. You don't want to accelerate too hard; otherwise, you could cause the bike to wheelie and the front wheel to jump out of the rut, which is another no-no that can get you in trouble.

You also want to keep an eye on the depth of the ruts you choose. If they get too deep, you could actually get stuck because the rut walls will start grabbing your chain guide, axles, and lower fork tubes. If you feel that a rut is getting dangerously deep, look for an alternative line; the odds are that there is one just a few feet away.

Line Selection

Regardless of whether you are turning on the flat or using a berm or rut to assist you in your search for traction, it's always best to experiment with as many lines as possible to see what works best.

"Look for the smoothest line around the corner that will offer you the best traction," insists Steve Lamson. "Stay away from bumps, if you can, and watch for mud or other things that could be slippery. Also, if you find that you have to cross ruts in a turn, it's best to cross them as perpendicularly as possible so they don't catch the sidewalls of your tires and cause you to lose control. Even if you don't crash, it will waste time and energy. You also want to avoid rocks or anything else that could cause either one of your wheels to break loose. If you hit something with your bike leaned over, it will be difficult to maintain control."

It is also critical that you avoid hard braking in any turn, unless you have to avoid a downed rider or something else dangerous. Jamming on the brakes will cause your wheels to slide, especially when you are leaned over; and if you are leaned over, the natural tendency will be to straighten up your bike and force it to go straight.

"Do all of your braking before the turn," says Mike Craig. "Most bikes turn better with the throttle on. If you brake in the turn, it may cause the bike to stand straight up."

Be sure to try several different lines through a turn. Even if one particular line is the fastest, you may find that you will need to take a different line to pass or to avoid a downed rider, or that a different line becomes faster as the track gets worn down.

All handling characteristics will change with the type of terrain and the type of traction. On slippery surfaces, such as hardpack and mud, you have to be less aggressive with both body position and throttle application. In sharp contrast, you can usually be more aggressive when it comes to riding in loam or sand.

Inside Lines

1. This is the same turn you saw Lamson rail the outside earlier, except this time he's snagging the inside line. The line is extremely difficult to get to because there is a small double jump immediately before the corner. To quickly brush off speed, Lamson actually lands short to use the second jump for resistance.

2. At this point Lamson finishes his braking and lines up his bike with the rut. The idea is to enter the rut as straight as possible so that both wheels align perfectly.

3. Swiftly, Lamson goes from standing to sitting in one quick motion and then drops his inside leg down for balance. Notice that his weight is on the furthermost portion of the seat, which helps load the front suspension, which in turn eventually helps provide more traction to the front tire.

CORNERING

- Most cornering is done in the seated position to lower the center of gravity.
- Weight the front of the bike to help the front wheel maintain traction.
- Train yourself to roll the throttle on when exiting corners, which will allow you to smooth your transition and start your drive earlier.
- Do most of your braking before initiating the turn.
- When possible, try to make wide, gradual turns to maintain momentum.
- Look for berms and ruts that could help you turn quicker, especially on off-camber turns.
- Try an assortment of lines.

4. As the rear wheel rolls into the groove, Lamson prepares to roll on the throttle. Throttle application must not be too aggressive or the rear wheel may jump out of the rut.

5. In this photo, Lamson has gotten back on the throttle. Notice how his weight is still forward, his inside foot is out with the toes angled up, and both elbows are up.

6. As he exits the turn, Lamson starts accelerating harder, yet keeps the same body positioning. Had there been acceleration bumps, he may have tried to wheelie them by sliding some of his weight back on the seat. In actuality, it wouldn't be a true wheelie, but rather just high enough so that the front wheel would skim over the top of the initial bumps so they wouldn't hamper steering.

7. The final stages of the turn show Lamson beginning to retract his foot and replace it on the footpeg.

Fundamental cornering skills are body position and coordinating the brakes and throttle. You should use the brakes until you get back on the throttle, feathering each during the transition. Using the brakes will also help you hold a line.

Remember: never coast. Brake or accelerate at all times and, occasionally, do both.

Brake to Turn

1. This reverse-angle sequence of Lamson taking the same inside line shows br[...] sliding and how using both brakes helps corner. In this shot, Lamson is hard on [...] brakes. Although his body position is forward, his torso is straight, keeping s[...] weight on the rear tire. Note that Lamson has lifted his heel off the right peg in o[...] to use the rear brake effectively while sitting down.

RELATED SECTIONS: BRAKING, ACCELERATION, STRATEGY

#23 OUTSIDE ELBOW UP

Raise your outside elbow above the handlebar when cornering. Your inside elbow should be a little lower.

If the outside elbow drops or is low while cornering, the rider has a tendency to twist his upper body toward the outside of the turn. This will prevent the rider from having proper leverage and will move the rider's body out of the center of balance.

In order to perform this technique correctly, overgrip the outside grip so you can keep your outside elbow high above the handlebar. Place your inside elbow in a neutral position that feels comfortable. Keep your shoul-ders facing toward the direction that you want to go and work your upper body from this framework in order to control the motorcycle and maintain the center of balance.

Stay in the center of balance and work the bike from there. Slide the bike and make it do what you want it to do. Don't try to lean and twist your body to the outside or hold the bike in position.

"The race is not always to the swift, but to those who keep running."

#24 INSIDE FOOT OUT

When cornering, put your inside foot out in front of you, very lightly sliding it on the ground, ready to lift the motorcycle up

straighter if it leans over too far. While doing this, keep some pressure on the outside footpeg.

The position of your inside foot while going through a corner is very important. Common mistakes include using the inside foot for a counterbalance and not using it to lift the motorcycle up if it tries to lean over too far or slide out. Common mistakes made with the outside foot include placing the arch of the foot on the footpeg instead of the ball of the foot, and resting it on the footpeg instead of pushing down on it.

In order to perform this technique correctly, your inside foot should be just barely skimming on the ground. It should be in a position that will give you a good shot at lifting up the motorcycle

2. Lamson has locked up the rear wheel and is initiating a brake-slide to turn the motorcycle. Note that his outside elbow is up and his shoulders are square to the bike. The front wheel is turned slightly left, anticipating the rear wheel slide. It also appears that he is applying light pressure to the front brake, which will hold the front end to a tighter line.

should the front wheel slide out. You do not want your hip, knee, and ankle to be locked, but you do need to have them stiff enough to hold the proper position. When you don't need that inside foot out there anymore, get it back on the footpeg as soon as possible.

While you're doing this, keep some pressure on the outside footpeg in order to maintain a low center of gravity, especially in flat corners without a berm. Like any other technique, practice this technique separately in order to develop your reflexes.

"Some people dream of worthy accomplishments, while others stay awake and do them."

#25 INSIDE FOOT TIMING

Put your inside foot out for the part of the turn where you're going from braking to accelerating (exit dex) and get it back on the footpeg as soon as possible.

Riders commonly make the mistake of putting their foot out too early to help them with balance. They are making the mistake of using their leg as a counterbalance. If you keep your shoulders square and your body centered, you don't need to use your leg as a counterbalance.

After making the corner, some riders also make the mistake of keeping their foot off the peg too long. This puts their weight on the seat, which makes those accelerating bumps beat their ass.

In order to perform this technique correctly, remove your foot from the footpeg for the least amount of time possible. Your foot should only be out during the part of the turn where you're switching from braking to accelerating. I call this part of the turn the exit dex. In other words, your foot should come out for this part of the turn and then get back on the footpeg as soon as possible. Keep your weight low, on the footpegs, and use the controls and your upper body movements for balance and control.

Practice this technique separately and you'll see how quickly it will begin to work for you. Timing, balance, and anticipation give you control.

"The difference between a successful person and others is not a lack of strength, not a lack of knowledge, but rather a lack of will."

3. The brake-slide has brought the bike into the main line. As soon as he gets off the brakes, Lamson is on the gas, as the slight roost tells us, and his inside leg is out, ready to catch a slide. His torso is leaned forward, weighting the front wheel to plant it in the rut.

#26 BRAKE OR ACCELERATE

When racing a motocross course, you should be either braking or accelerating, never coasting. Sometimes you will do a little of each at the same time.

Now we're getting into the more advanced technical stuff that takes a lot of time and practice on the motorcycle. But this is what it takes to go fast and be in control.

Beginner riders are either braking, accelerating, or coasting. They usually do these things separately. They are missing the benefit of not only controlling the speed and momentum of the motorcycle, but also the way the motorcycle handles and holds the track.

A pro rider has developed such a fine feel and manipulation of all the controls that he can operate them all at the same time with perfect control of each one.

Many times when transitioning from braking to accelerating and from accelerating to braking, a pro will feather the clutch and throttle and the front and rear brakes at the same time. And even when he is not feathering them, he is going from one straight to the other. There is no coasting.

"The only limit to our realization of tomorrow will be our doubts of today."

#27 APPROACH DEX

The approach dex is where you go from accelerating to braking. There should be no coasting in between.

You will find an approach dex anytime you come upon an obstacle that causes you to make a transition from accelerating to braking. These can be found entering corners, before certain jumps, entering whoops, on downhills and drop-offs, and so on.

Beginner riders typically need improvement here. Beginners tend to go from accelerating to coasting then braking and then usually some more coasting and braking again.

The correct technique is to go straight from accelerating to braking. Many times accelerating and braking will overlap. This makes the bike handle better and gives you more control over the situation.

Don't panic brake; practice smooth, controlled braking.

"The mind is the limit. As long as the mind can envision the fact that you can do something, you can do it, as long as you believe 100 percent."
—Arnold Schwarzenegger

#28 EXIT DEX

The exit dex is where you go from braking to accelerating. Again, there should be no coasting in between.

This is similar to technique #27, but now we're talking about a different transition. The exit dex is most often found in corners. The common mistake here is going from braking to coasting, then to accelerating. This mistake will make the front wheel more likely to slide out.

4. On the exit, Lamson dials the throttle on. The front wheel is canted left a bit, indicating Lamson is relying on a slight rear wheel slide to bring the wheels in line and give him a straight drive out of the corner.

In some corners you should go from hard braking to hard accelerating, but more often you're going from hard braking (coming into the corner) to lighter and lighter braking, until you begin to lightly accelerate, then after that, you accelerate hard. This means that the transition between braking and accelerating always has to be controlled, whether it's hard or light. Most of the time braking and accelerating will overlap.

There's a lot more to motocross than guts and glory. It's more like precision and control.

"Knowing that you have complete control of your thinking, you will recognize the power."

#29 CONNECT THE DEXES

During the approach dex and the exit dex make smooth transitions from accelerating to braking and from braking to accelerating. You need to blend the forces of

braking and/or accelerating together just how and when you want with the use of the controls. This requires mastery of all five controls.

Yes, we are still talking about the approach dex and the exit dex. This is because they are such important parts of motocross racing. One of the reasons they are important is that there is a big transition between the approach dex (accelerating to braking) and the exit dex (braking to accelerating). Because of this big transition it's necessary to have perfect control the whole time. If you control the front and rear brakes and the gearshift, clutch, and throttle properly, you will have control. This is because the proper use of these controls makes the motorcycle handle a certain way according to how you're using them. For instance, when you're leaning the motorcycle over coming into a corner and you're dragging the rear brake, it pulls the front wheel back and to the inside. This will keep the

front wheel from sliding out. As soon as you let go of the rear brake, you'd better be on the gas to maintain control, because if you coast, that's when the front wheel will slide out. That's only one example; there are several more. Just remember, accelerating or braking, never coasting.

"We can know what people are thinking by looking at what they do. Actions mirror thoughts. And by taking a good look at where we are and what we are doing, we can understand what we are thinking. The thoughts we have chosen have brought us to where we are today."

#30 FEATHER THE FRONT BRAKE

Feathering the front brake while going through a bermed corner will hold the front wheel in the berm and make the motorcycle turn sharper.

The common mistake when entering bermed corners is letting go of the

5. Again, Lamson is set up for a good drive. Note, however, that his wheels are not in line to drive out of the corner, as he is still pointed a bit wide. At this point, he needs to keep turning left. In consideration of that, he will probably keep power application smooth and moderate by using the clutch and throttle. Once the bike is in the groove and pointed in the right direction, Lamson will open up and drive hard to the next obstacle.

front brake too soon. The rider thinks he is slowed down enough for the berm, so he releases the front brake. When the brake is released, the front wheel will tend to go over the berm.

A pro will keep his finger on the front brake until he opens the throttle. Then he will automatically let go of the front brake. This means he has the ability to feather the front brake until he is ready to exit the berm hard.

When you're leaning over in a berm and you apply the front brake, it shortens the steering angle, slows the motorcycle down, and makes it turn sharper. The benefit is that you can come into the berms faster and still stay in the berm. This is especially true in right-hand corners because you have to let go of the rear brake in order to put your foot out for the corner.

Learn to feather that front brake and throttle together through the exit dex (the transition between braking and acceleration) in bermed corners and you will never go over a berm again.

"Every failure brings with it the seed of an equivalent success."
—Napoleon Hill

#31 BRAKE/THROTTLE COORDINATION

You can feather the front brake and throttle at the same time.

Use one finger on the front brake.

This is similar to the previous technique. Many techniques in motocross work together to give you overall control. In this case, we're talking about the control that you will have when you learn to feather the front brake and throttle together. This is done most often in bermed corners.

Many riders use only one control at a time. For example, they let go of the front brake before they begin to use the throttle. A rider will not be in total con-

trol of the situation with this crude use of the controls. Also, some beginner riders use two, three, or even four fingers on the front brake. This is not good because they won't be able to hold on to the throttle as well. With disc brakes, one finger is all you need.

As we talked about earlier, you have to be able to control your speed and momentum at all times, especially at the approach dex and exit dex (the transitions from acceleration to braking and vice versa). One of the ways to do this is to have the ability to control both the front brake and throttle at the same time. Of course, you would not use the front brake and throttle hard at the same time. By feathering the front brake and throttle at the same time, you have total control of your speed and momentum through the critical exit dex. This control also makes the motorcycle turn sharper and better.

If you're going to ride better, you're going to have to master these more precise techniques. The only way to do so is to practice.

"It sometimes seems that intense desire creates not only its own opportunities, but its own talents."

#32 FRONT BRAKE USE DURING BRAKE-SLIDES

When brake-sliding into a corner, use the front brake to target your pivot.

You can use the front brake as hard as you need to in this situation, because while the motorcycle is brake-sliding, the front wheel is tracking straight and will not slide out.

The front brake has more stopping power than the rear brake. Many riders lock up the rear brake in the corner in order to do a brake-slide, but they let go of the front brake way too early. When this happens they have little control of where they pivot their brake-slide because the motorcycle is just sliding in the turn. They have no stopping power.

When the motorcycle is brake-sliding you can still use the front brake. The front wheel will be tracking straight and will not slide out. This way you can come into the corner much faster and deeper and still pivot your brake-slide exactly where you want it.

Master using all the controls at the same time. Not just one at a time.

"Nothing stops the man who desires to achieve. Every obstacle is simply a course to develop his achievement muscle. It's a strengthening of his powers of accomplishment."

#33 BRAKE-SLIDE TO ACCELERATION

End your brake-slide where you want to turn, and use the clutch, throttle, and brakes to go from brake-slide to power slide in one fluid motion.

When you want to square off a corner with a brake-slide and exit in a power slide, the brake-slide is the easy part. Heck, even little kids on their bicycles can do brake-slides. The tricky part is to pick up the power slide just before the brake-slide finishes off. If this is not done correctly, the motorcycle will hesitate and do just about everything except what you want it to do.

Make sure you brake-slide deep enough into the corner. When you're finished with your brake-slide, you should be at least halfway around the corner. This way you'll be facing the right way when you begin the power slide. Make sure your timing of letting go of the brakes and starting the power slide with the clutch and throttle is precise and controlled.

Practice making this transition on different surfaces, from tacky to slick.

"Through some strange and powerful principle of 'mental chemistry' which she has never divulged, Nature wraps up in the impulse of strong desire, 'that something' which recognizes no such word as 'impossible,' and accepts no such reality as failure."

—Napoleon Hill

Running in Too Deep

If you run into a turn a little too deep, you need to try not to panic. In this photo, Jimmy Button overshot the corner and concentrated on making the corner anyway. Notice that his rear wheel is actually over the berm, but Button's proper body positioning allows him to fix the problem rather easily.

#34 BRAKE FOR CONTROL

Use the rear brake when entering a corner to hold the front wheel back and to the inside, keeping it from sliding out.

As we covered earlier, letting go of the front brake too early takes away your control. The same holds true with the rear brake.

The common mistake a rider makes here is letting go of the rear brake when entering a corner. This eliminates the rider's ability to slow down before the bike is facing the exit of the corner. This means they have to slow down early and give up control at the critical exit dex.

Your hardest braking should take place when you first shut the throttle off for the corner. This is where you need to scrub off the most speed quickly. Then as you get farther into the corner you brake lighter and lighter all the way to the exit dex (where you go from braking to accelerating), where you finally let go of the brakes completely as you get on the clutch and throttle hard.

You'll feel the control when you learn to feather the rear brake to this point. No precision, no control.

"The starting point of all achievement is desire. Keep this constantly in mind. Weak desires bring weak results, just as a small amount of fire makes a small amount of heat."

—Napoleon Hill

Chapter 8

JUMPS
The Search for Air

Few will argue that jumping a motorcycle is one of the most fun things in life. The sensation is incredible and it's usually why riders choose off-road to street riding or road racing.

As you will discover, there are all types of obstacles used for grabbing air, including everything from extremely slow-speed kickers to drop-offs to wide-open, top-speed jumps. Combine these with tabletop and combination jumps, such as doubles or triples, and you can see that there are many ways to initiate flight.

Jumps, however, require much caution since they have the ability to painfully punish riders for even very minor mistakes. That's precisely why it is so critical to ride within your own limits at all times and resist the urge to become a daredevil.

The single most important thing to remember when learning to jump is to start with small obstacles. Make sure that you are really comfortable jumping before you move on to larger obstacles.

Secondly, learn on single jumps. Do not attempt tabletop, double, triple, or any combination jump until you feel that you have mastered single jumping.

With this in mind, successful jumping depends on several key factors such as body position, timing, throttle and clutch control, bike setup, and realistic jump choice.

When learning to jump, it's always a good idea to experiment with different techniques. Try front- and rear-wheel landings at slow speeds, and only try larger jumps when you have a good idea of how the bike will react to different jump faces, landing areas, terrain types, and dirt consistencies. There are hundreds of thousands of variables in the world of motocross and off-road riding, and jumps are one of the most difficult obstacles to master. This is John Dowd using the bump-seat technique to get a little more lift than he would achieve with the normal attack body position.

Feeling comfortable while jumping is important at all times. Steve Lamson is one of the best jumpers in the world and his style is proof that he feels very relaxed.

Changing Conditions

All tracks change throughout the course of the day, and one of the most vulnerable areas are jump faces. Watch out for kickers like these deep ruts and always look for smoother lines while riding.

Look Before You Leap

Every jump should begin with careful analysis of the obstacle. Study the approach and look for any acceleration bumps, rocks, dirt clods, ruts, or anything else that could interfere with you, your bike, and its suspension. Then study the face of the jump. Look for any lips that could kick you off balance, or holes that could wreak havoc with your suspension. From there, inspect the landing area and look for a realistic location to land. Finally, before jumping, roll over the obstacle a few times to get your bearings.

"Before you jump you should always be familiar with your surroundings," Jeremy McGrath says. "You should always know where you want to land; otherwise, you increase your chances of getting hurt."

After you have analyzed the jump and rolled over it a few times, you should have a fairly good understanding of how and at what angle it will toss you into flight. Your talent for making this determination will become much more clearly defined with experience.

Body Position

Most jumps require you to reposition your body several times to maintain proper balance at all times. That's why the generally preferred body position is standing with your weight centered, your knees and elbows bent, and your eyes focused ahead. This will help you make sudden movements on the bike and will help you soak up the impact of the jump more effectively.

Ideally, any movement to reposition your body should be done in a smooth motion. Though speed is sometimes necessary, finesse is very important; otherwise, your own movements could upset the balance further.

Landing Attitude

On standard jumps where you are landing on flat ground, the usual goal is to land both wheels at the same time. At higher speeds, however, most riders find it better to land with the front wheel approximately 6 inches higher than the rear. This will reduce headshake upon impact, because the shock will hit first, and will reduce the likelihood of the front wheel wanting to wash out. Another variable would be a turn immediately after the jump that would usually warrant a front wheel landing at slow (i.e., safe)

Jumping Fundamentals

1. A small jump is a good place to learn how a bike reacts. In this sequence, Danny Carlson demonstrates the fundamentals of jumping by standing up with his knees bent, foot on the brake, arms up, elbows bent, and eyes focused ahead.

2. As Carlson lifts off the ground, he uses his weight to balance the bike. He pushes out on the handlebar slightly to keep the front end from rising, and weights the rear portion of the bike so it doesn't kick him over the handlebar.

3. Carlson holds the position until he feels that a correction needs to be made. If the front wheel were to rise he may have to shift his weight forward. Conversely, if the front wheel were to suddenly drop, he might have pulled up on the handlebar. If more drastic measures are required, he may hit the rear brake to drop the front or gas it to spin the rear wheel and drop the rear wheel.

speeds. During front wheel landings, you want the front wheel to land about 6 inches lower than the rear wheel.

When landing front wheel first, a technique that is rarely used, it is usually best to have your weight over the back of the seat and to stay off the front brake. This, along with a good stance that allows your knees and elbows to soak up the jolt, will reduce the chances of endoing.

Uphill and downhill landings usually warrant a flat style of landing where both wheels come in contact with the ground at the same time. When there is a question of landing approach on single jumps, it is usually best to allow the rear wheel to touch down first.

Throughout all stages of the jump, the standing position allows the rider to control the attitude of the bike by pushing and pulling on the handlebar, which allows the bike to pivot somewhat on the footpeg axis while simultaneously moving rider weight forward or backwards. The photos will illustrate this point.

"If you accidentally jump front wheel low, you can sometimes get the bike to level out a little by pinning the throttle," Danny Carlson says. "The gyroscopic effect of the rear wheel has a lot of control over the bike. This is also why some riders tap the rear brake in the air to lower the front wheel. This also requires pulling in the clutch and giving the bike a few safety revs so it doesn't stall in midair when the brake is activated."

"When I land I usually try to match the angle of the bike with the ground, except in rough sections where I'll keep the front wheel about half a foot high so the fork doesn't twist," says Ron Lechien. "If you land in a rough area with both wheels at the same time you'll lose a lot of drive as the fork and shock rebound. If you land rear wheel first with the throttle on, the shock won't spring back up so quickly and you should get a better drive."

"Unless you're landing uphill, or accidentally coming up short on a double jump, don't let the front wheel come up too high," says John Dowd. "The higher the front wheel gets, the harder it will slam down when you land."

It is also very important that you weight both footpegs equally so that you don't upset the bike's balance. Until you get into advanced jumping techniques, the idea is to keep the bike straight up and down and not leaned over to one side. A bike leaning over

4. As Carlson lands, he repositions his body toward the middle of the bike and soaks up the impact with his knees and elbows. Landing with the throttle on will ease the impact and get the bike driving as soon as possible.

5. Carlson holds the throttle on momentarily, allowing the engine to help maintain forward momentum, which is critical in helping the suspension absorb the energy. Had he wanted to brake immediately, the suspension would have undergone more strain and dipped further into the travel, perhaps even bottomed out.

will have an increased chance of causing the wheels to wash out on the jump face or the landing area, which could cause an assortment of unpleasant events. If this happens in the air, it may be corrected by adding additional weight to the footpeg that is higher, but this is a technique that should be used only when necessary.

Tabletops

Once you feel comfortable with single jumps, you may be ready to start jumping tabletops. This obstacle is like a double jump, but it's usually much safer because the consequences of coming up short usually aren't as severe. Once again the idea is to start off small and work your way to larger tabletop jumps.

After careful inspection and rolling the jump a few times, you should try to land on top of the tabletop so you can get an idea of how the jump will toss you and start getting a good idea of how much speed will be required to clear the entire jump and land on the downslope. Continue landing on top, each time jumping a little farther (at a pace you feel comfortable with), until you start coming close to the end. You'll know when you are

getting close because your suspension will bounce you off the end of the jump as it rebounds, and you won't have time to brake until you land at the very base of the jump.

In most cases the idea is to jump front wheel high (about 6 inches higher than the rear wheel). This will give you greater control over the bike in case you realize that you have under- or overjumped the obstacle. Ideally, if you matched your pace and think that you will land on the downslope, you should push forward on the handlebar to begin lowering the front end of the bike (as you push forward on the handlebar your weight should

Double Jumps

1. Double jumps are a frequently used component of modern-day tracks. The idea is to jump over the second obstacle and land on its backside. Small jumps like these offer the best way to develop the skills needed for this advanced technique. In this photo, Steve Lamson approaches the jump with just enough speed to clear the space between the two jumps.

2. In the previous photo, Lamson had his weight centered, but notice how he shifted his body to the back of the bike. This is actually the result of pushing on the handlebar to lower the front end. When the landing area is on a downward slope, it's usually preferred to match the attitude of the bike with the landing zone.

move slightly forward, which will add additional influence to the bike's attitude). Most riders usually prefer to have their bike parallel to the ground at the midpoint of the jump, and then slowly dip the front wheel during the later stages of flight.

In most instances the idea is to match the bike angle to the landing ramp, which usually provides a soft landing. This is the same approach that Alpine skiers use on the massive 100-plus meter jumps where they descend several stories. If a man jumped 50 feet straight down and landed on flat ground the odds are that the end result could be tragic. However, when landing on a downslope, the energy absorption characteristics are

much better because you decelerate at a slower pace.

If you feel that you are going to come up short and "case it" then you usually want to hit the end of the tabletop with both wheels at the same time so that you have more control over the bike. If you were to land front wheel first, you wouldn't be able to get a good drive (using the motor's power) to maintain control of the bike. If you overjump the tabletop, it is usually preferable to land in the same manner, totally flat with the throttle on.

Fly Low

After you feel confident with tabletop jumps you can try altering your technique. "On

tabletop jumps I always try to stay as low as possible," says Danny Carlson. "After I know I have enough momentum to clear the jump, I chop the throttle on the face of the jump, but only about the last two or three feet of it, and then push the handlebar forward once my front wheel lifts off the ground. I do this in one motion that causes my whole body to shift. The object is to redirect the bike so it's going forward instead of upwards."

Doubles

If there ever comes a point in your life where you feel confident attempting double jumps, you should approach them in the same fashion as tabletop jumps. Be forewarned,

3. Before touching down, Lamson repositions his body once again so that his weight returns to the center. Notice that he is still standing in the attack position.

however, that the penalty for underjumping them is oftentimes much more severe than coming up short on a tabletop.

When possible, practice single jumping even to the point that you are almost landing at the base of the second jump (unless it's too big a leap—you be the judge). Single-jump practicing will once again be the best way to determine speed and to get a good idea of trajectory. Only after you feel totally confident and ready should you attempt a double jump.

"Double jumping requires total commitment," says Steve Lamson. "You have to give it 100 percent effort. Once you are in the air, there's no going back."

The angle of the bike on takeoff, in the air and on landing should be the same if you have calculated your distance correctly, and you will, in fact, land on the downside of the jump. When in doubt, it's usually better to overjump than underjump, because the penalties are generally less painful and severe. It all depends on the landing area and how much room you have before the next obstacle.

While overjumping doubles requires the same technique as overjumping tabletops, underjumping is much different. It's usually best to land front wheel high if you are coming up way short and plan to land on the face of the jump. The impact will be very severe and this method will allow both the fork

and the shock to take the hit simultaneously. If you are going to case it—that is, land with one wheel on either side of the jump—you should do so with the bike parallel to the ground. If you case it with the front wheel lower than the rear, there's a good chance you'll endo. If you land front wheel high, the rear suspension will rebound wildly and could cause you to do a number of strange things, none of which are good.

"When you're learning how to double jump, start out small and then work your way up," says Danny Carlson. "It's also a good idea to find jumps to practice on where the second one is rounded so the consequences won't be so bad if you come up short."

4. As both wheels touch down, Lamson absorbs some of the shock with his knees and elbows, but remains standing. In this particular jump, the shock wasn't that severe, so the suspension wasn't affected too much.

Triple Jumps

Triples require the same approach as doubles—that is, you work up to them. Begin by rolling the jumps, then landing between the first two, then double, then overjump the double (if possible) until you feel like tripling. Once you triple, pretend the middle jump doesn't exist and treat it like a long double.

Elevated Doubles

Another type of double or triple incorporates an uphill, where the intent is to ascend to a different elevation. In this instance, you continue working up to the jump at your own pace, but once you decide to commit, the idea is usually to match the angle of the landing area, which in most cases will be flat.

Matching the angle is the same idea used for downhill double or triple jumps; however, the penalty for jumping short will be intensified since it's much more difficult to lose momentum when traveling downhill. If you clip the final jump with either wheel, it will be extremely difficult to control the angle of the bike.

Drop-Offs

One of the final types of jumps is the drop-off. Typically you should strive to land with the front wheel 6 to 12 inches off the ground, which will allow the suspension to work its best. In most instances, the landing area of drop-offs will be filled with chuckholes caused by the erratic acceleration of previous bikes that have landed all over the place. The acceleration will help

your suspension absorb the impact through more efficient energy absorption.

"Front-wheel landings are usually only a good idea when landing on smooth ground that won't mess with your suspension," says Lamson. "Most of the time front-wheel landings are only used when you have to get on the brakes quickly after a jump, or on the downside of a double, triple, or tabletop jump where a corner or another obstacle immediately follows."

If you are jumping in an area that is difficult to judge, Mike Healey has a suggestion. "On blind jumps where I can't see the landing area on the approach, I always try to find reference points so I make sure I land in the right area. Most of the time I'll follow the line that's been worked into the ground, but sometimes

Kicker Jumps

Watch out for kicker jumps because their natural tendency is to kick riders over the handlebar. In essence, kicker jumps are short, steep-faced jumps and bumps that toss the rear wheel substantially higher into the air than the front wheel. The preferred technique to master these is to approach the jump at a slow to moderate speed while standing up with most of your body weight toward the rear of the seat. The faster you hit the jump the more severe the kicking effect. Once you come into contact with the jump, accelerate all the way off its face in order to keep the front wheel high. On the face, you should try to provide resistance to the rear suspension by not allowing your knees to flex on the jump face. If you attempt to soak up the jump with your knees, the effects of the shock rebounding will increase, and so will the likelihood of you going over the handlebars. It's important, however, that you don't lock your knees—you want to make sure you can move them if you need to reposition your weight at a moment's notice.

Be extremely careful on rut-filled approaches. Here Tallon Vohland sits back on his bike to allow his front end to settle into the rut as he drives off this high-speed double.

I have to use trees, rocks, or other land markings for reference."

Sitting Down on the Job

While standing is the most widely used body position for jumping, there are times when sitting may be preferred. At times, sitting on takeoff can be an effective means of jumping, because it can provide additional lift, but sitting should only be done if the conditions are perfect. It requires a smooth, bump-free approach to the jump and a gradual jump face. Sitting down will usually cause the bike to be tossed higher and farther off the jump because it doesn't allow your knees to soak up any of the shock on takeoff; therefore, the suspension is compressed further on the jump face and then generally rebounds quicker on takeoff. The quicker rebound is one of the key factors that ultimately determines height and distance.

Regardless of the type of jump, it's important that you are very familiar with your engine's power characteristics so that your bike doesn't do anything unexpected. If you are tackling an uphill double or triple jump and your bike can't produce enough drive, it is important that you know that beforehand.

"Keep a finger on the clutch in case the bike bogs at any time, especially when you land," Lechien recommends. "If you're landing on an uphill or if you naturally lose a lot of momentum in the air, you may have to downshift before you land so you can continue your drive."

Ultimately, good jumping depends on rider skill and how well you can read the terrain so you can alter your technique appropriately.

JUMPS

- Start with small jumps at slow speeds.
- In most instance maintain a neutral body position on the bike.
- Typically the idea is to stand on takeoff, in midair, and while landing.
- Adjust your body position in the air to control the attitude of the bike.
- Use your knees and elbows to help the suspension absorb the impact.
- Use the motor's acceleration to help the suspension soak up energy while landing.
- Landing on downslopes is typically much easier on the suspension and the rider.
- Avoid landing with the brakes on whenever possible.
- If you are in the air for an extended period of time, rev the engine as much as necessary to keep it from stalling.
- When jumping double, triple, or tabletop jumps, the usual goal is to land on the downslope and avoid clipping the top portion of the landing area.

From Approach to Landing

1. Before any double, triple, or tabletop jump, the approach is always pivotal for success. In order to clear the jump you need to have enough acceleration, which usually requires a straight, bump-free run at the takeoff jump.

2. On the jump face, the suspension will absorb some of the impact, which can be seen here as Steve Lamson nearly bottoms the rear end. On takeoff, it's important to have the engine in the powerband, keep your body weight centered, and stand up so you can use your knees to soak up some of the shock.

3. To get the best drive, Lamson accelerates all the way off the face of the jump. This, in turn, will naturally cause the front end to rise faster than the rear. To balance out this effect, Lamson pushes away on the handlebar slightly, which also shifts his weight to the back of the seat. This allows the bike to pivot on the footpeg axis.

4. In the air it's best to stay a little loose so that you can adjust the attitude of the bike if needed. In most cases it's best to use finesse instead of muscle to control the flight pattern.

5. As Lamson prepares to land he begins to readjust the altitude of the bike to match the downslope of the landing area. Once again he has pushed down on the handlebar, causing his weight to slide back even further.

6. As the front end drops rapidly, Lamson's butt begins to touch the rear portion of the seat. Though it appears that he's sitting, Lamson is actually still standing.

7. A split second before touching down, Lamson returns his body to the centered position so that he is standing with his knees and elbows bent to absorb the impact. This particular uphill triple jump is followed by a corner, so Lamson has to brake instead of accelerate.

Drop-Offs

1. Drop-off jumps can be tricky because the end result is usually a harsh impact. The idea is to go off the jump with your weight toward the back of the bike in the standing—but crouched—position. As the bike drops, the idea is to extend your legs to maintain control of the bike. It's also wise to jump front wheel high because it provides more control upon landing.

2. You can see how John Dowd has extended his knees to handle the effects of the sudden drop. Notice that his front wheel is approximately 6 inches higher than the rear and that his body is close to the attack position.

3. The harsh landing is softened as Dowd collapses his knees and elbows. As the roost indicates, he's hard on the throttle, which will also soften the blow through the use of increased forward momentum. This forward momentum technique is the same thing that allows Alpine ski jumpers to soar over 100 meters and drop several stories without the use of any suspension.

4. Immediately after landing, Dowd continues to accelerate to the next obstacle in the standing attack position.

JUMPS

The emphasis on jumping in motocross cannot be overstated. Supercross is all about jumping and timing, and motocross tracks have changed to incorporate Supercross-style obstacles. To win today, you must master the air as well as the earth.

The key to controlling the jump is at takeoff. By using the correct technique and practicing until jumping is natural and relaxed, you can have complete control over your airborne machine.

Combination Jumps

1. **Some tracks feature combination jumps. Though combination jumps come in all shapes, sizes, and styles, this particular one consists of a set of ascending whoops before a double jump.**

RELATED SECTIONS: WHOOPS, STRATEGY

#35 JUMP HIGHER

To jump higher and farther, load the suspension just before take-off and help it unload on takeoff.

Be careful when practicing this technique. Start off small and work your way up gradually as you gain confidence and control.

The most common mistake here is for the rider to tense up or freeze at the most critical part of the jump, which occurs upon compression and rebound as the motorcycle leaves the ground. By freezing, the rider is left at the mercy of inertia.

The correct way to jump is to use your body weight to help the suspension compress just before it starts to rebound. Then you want to help the suspension rebound by lifting your weight out of the suspension just as it begins to rebound. At the same time, adjust the angle of your upper body to control the height of the front wheel as the motorcycle is in the air.

Remember that the most important part of the jump is the part where the motorcycle actually leaves the ground. What is going to happen at this point? You guessed it, compression and rebound. Rather than tensing up, key into it and go with the flow. It feels good and you won't have to change your shorts as often.

"Repetition is the mother of skill."

#36 JUMP LOWER

Absorb the compression and rebound part of the jump with your body when you want less height and distance on a jump. Let the motorcycle come up under you by giving a little in your elbows and knees.

Most beginning riders don't know the difference between jumping far and high, or jumping short and low in order to get back on the ground quickly and gain time. They just jump with the same technique and style every time. There is definitely a big difference in these two techniques.

To jump shorter and lower you want to help the motorcycle absorb the compression and rebound part of the jump with your body movements. You want to suck the bike up under you when you jump. This way you can cover the jumps faster and still get back on the ground smoother and quicker.

Practice both ways and you will definitely notice a big difference. Of course, practice on a safe jump.

2. In jumps like this, confidence and timing are everything. Had Mike Craig not landed in the right place, he may have gotten a bad suspension bounce and/or lost his drive to successfully clear the small double jump at the end.

#37 AERIAL ADJUSTMENTS

While the motorcycle is airborne, pulling in the clutch and locking up the rear wheel will make the front wheel drop slightly. Grabbing a handful of throttle will make the front wheel rise slightly.

Although the most important part of the jump is where the motorcycle leaves the ground, you still have to control it through the air in order to set up for your landing. As with the launch, you need to be relaxed and loose in the air. Don't be a panic jumper.

Once the bike is in the air, you can control it to a degree with your body. In addition, the clutch and throttle can give you some interesting gyroscopic effects.

You can drop the front end slightly by pulling in the clutch and hitting the rear brake in order to lock up the rear wheel. By suddenly stopping the spinning force of the rear wheel the front end will drop. The faster the rear wheel is spinning, the more the front will drop.

By grabbing a handful of throttle and suddenly spinning the rear wheel faster, the front wheel will rise. This is called panic revving, because you've got your front wheel too low and you don't care how much noise you're making as long as you save it.

It's not a good idea to lock up the front wheel while airborne. Oh yeah, it will drop the front end, but it can cause a squirrelly landing because the front wheel will still be stopped when you land.

So you see, the controls of the motorcycle are still important even when the wheels are in the air.

3. Craig executed this entire jump perfectly. Notice how his front wheel is about 6 inches higher than the rear during the first half of flight. If he comes up short, Craig will maintain the stance to help the suspension soak up the impact more efficiently; however, Craig did, in fact, have enough momentum so that he was able to readjust his body position and eventually match his angle with the downslope of the final jump.

#38 TURNING IN THE AIR

When you want to turn the motorcycle in the air, lean, turn, and whip the rear end over as you take off the jump. While you're in the air, maintain the center of balance and straighten it out before you land.

You may have seen some beginner riders trying to whip it sideways through the air and all that ends up happening is they turn the front wheel.

When you want to throw it sideways, you have to set up as you approach the jump. The most important part happens as the motorcycle leaves the jump. You have to lean, turn, and whip it as you take off. Then you have to maintain the center of balance with your body positions and movements while you make adjustments through the air. If you're having trouble straightening it up upon landing, it's most likely because you're not maintaining the center of balance with your body movements.

You pretty much have to commit yourself to how much you're going to lean over and sideways as you leave the jump. This technique can be fairly dangerous, so be very careful. Practice step by step on a good safe takeoff and landing. A big step-up jump is the safest.

Although this technique is mostly for show, it does have other benefits.

You can set up for a corner in the air and can be turning as you land. Also, this technique can prepare you for the inevitable time when you come off a jump out of shape.

Nowadays, just riding on the ground is not enough. You have to be able to fly, too.

"Where there is a will there is a way, is an old and true saying. He who resolves upon doing a thing, by that very resolution often scales the barriers to do it, and secures its achievement. To think we are able, is almost to be so. To determine upon attainment is frequently attainment itself."

This rider has come up short and has landed on top of the third jump of this triple. Fortunately, he's using the proper technique and is trying to absorb most of the impact with his knees and elbows, which act as additional suspension.

Rear-wheel landings are usually not preferred on big jumps because they make the fork feel harsher than flat landings on the downslope. This is called a "slap down" and usually happens when riders adjust their bodies when they feel they will come up short. If you do come up short, this may be one of the only techniques that can save you from disaster. Then again, it's never pleasant to come up short.

1. This rider has come up way short on the same triple jump. Had he landed flat or with his front wheel first, he probably would have endoed. As it is, he's still going to experience a wild ride.

2. Upon the initial impact, the suspension has bottomed hard and has rebounded him extremely fast. This has sent his bike and body into an endo, and all he can do is reposition his body to the back of the bike and hang on.

3. The endo starts to worsen. It's very important to stay off the front brake in situations like this.

4. This is one of the most critical points in the rider's attempt to save himself from crashing. He needs to keep his weight on the back of the bike, but is having a difficult time.

5. At this point the rider starts to lose his battle. His arms start to buckle and his body starts to move forward on the bike. Because of this he eventually endoed, but the rest of the sequence occurred out of camera range.

Chapter 9

RUTS
Mind Over Matter

Ruts are unlike any other obstacle you will encounter. The nature of deep channels typically gives riders the least amount of control over their motorcycle while still being "in control." More or less, once both tires drop down into a narrow groove you are just along for the ride and can do very little to make a direction change. In fact, you can do more harm than good. If you try to change direction, you'll probably end up out of shape or on the ground. If you relax and ride with the rut, you'll be just fine.

Though ruts are usually unpleasant and cause riders a lot of grief, there are some strategies to make them much easier and more user friendly.

"Always scan ahead to see where the rut leads and if it branches out into other lines," says Guy Cooper. "If you aren't paying attention you could wind up getting stuck or led way out of your way."

"Monitor the ruts around the entire track to see how rapidly they're getting deeper," instructs John Dowd. "You'll be surprised at how fast good lines can deteriorate; therefore, you've got to keep a sharp eye out for better lines."

Careful rut analysis is very important and is the first step toward successful completion. In many cases, there will be alternative rut-free lines available that would normally be considered out of the way. But when you do have to ride ruts, there are other things you have to remember.

Ruts can be intimidating, but can be conquered with proper knowledge and good technique. The key is confidence and technique.

"The goal with any rut is to enter the line as straight as possible so you can flow with the line," says Guy Cooper. "You want to make sure that both wheels can smoothly get into the groove, thus helping you maintain the most control over your bike. If you get the front wheel in but the back end is still out, or vice versa, then you'll be cross-rutted. When you're cross-rutted you aren't able to maintain total control, which will cripple your speed and possibly cause you to crash."

"I have found that there is not a single universal riding style that works well for riding ruts all the time," adds Cooper. "However, I have found that keeping the front end light in straight-aways and not fighting the bike seems to work the best. In turns, I've learned that a less aggressive approach works well, but the real trick is line selection."

"In ruts that are really deep, you have to be careful that your lower fork tubes don't get caught in the rut," instructs Steve Lamson. "The same thing can happen with your footpegs, swingarm, and chain guide. If any one of these scrape too much, it will rob you of momentum and will possibly cause you to crash."

Good rut-riding skills can make the difference between finishing or having to push your bike off the track. Ruts can also be turned to your advantage, either for passing or to hold a clean line.

"In deep ruts, try to keep your toes pointed upwards so they don't snag on the rut walls. If your foot catches, it will instantly rip your foot off the bike, and there's nothing you can do about it."

Typically, you will find that you will have to go slower than normal while driving in ruts. This is due to the fact that you will have a more difficult time trying to maintain your balance.

"Try to stay fluid on the bike," recommends Ron Lechien. "Any abrupt movements could cause you to lose your balance. This is definitely one place where finesse pays off."

"Before you enter a rut it is usually a good idea to make sure that you have finished all of your braking," says Mike Healey. "I'm not saying that you can't brake while you are in a rut; you have to do it every once in a while, I'm just saying that you will have less control and the front end is more likely to twist."

Plan Your Attack

1. When approaching a series of ruts, it's important to carefully analyze the situation. Choose the shallowest groove that provides the straightest shot to the next obstacle. In this sequence, Mike Craig is using finesse to get a smooth launch off the jump.

2. Instead of turning the bike to correct a balance problem, Craig simply shifts his body to the right in the second photo. While in the rut, let the bike ride in it naturally (rather than climb out of the rut) and concentrate on the obstacle ahead. Work the wheel slightly left and right, adjusting to keep the front wheel in the center of the rut.

Railing Ruts

When used effectively, ruts can actually be the hot ticket around a turn because they provide resistance, which serves the same purpose as bankings in automotive racing. Here, Mike LaRocco rails the turn with surgical perfection and gets so much traction that he is able to wheelie while leaning way over.

Rutted Corners

1. In this sequence James Dobb enters the rutted turn perfectly and at the proper speed. All of his braking was done well in advance. Notice that his elbows are up, his inside foot is out for balance, his eyes are focused ahead, and he appears to be in total control. What you can't see is that Dobb is weighting his outside footpeg, which helps the bike stay balanced.

2. Dobb continues to make a gradual arch and hasn't changed his body position. At this point he's rolling on the throttle slowly in order to rocket out of the turn. A word of caution: too much throttle or clutch action could cause the front wheel to jump out of the line and spoil the perfect turn.

3. Dobb is accelerating hard, as evidenced by the slight wheelie. Notice that the bike is actually oversteering as his suspension rebounds upon the exit. Also notice that Dobb has shifted his weight farther forward in a very aggressive manner.

RUTS

- Look for alternative lines.
- Scan ahead to see where the rut leads.
- In a straight line, choose the straightest rut possible.
- Pay attention to see how the ruts deteriorate over time.
- Avoid following other riders in the same rut when possible.
- Watch out for the chain guide, fork tubes, footpegs, gear shifter, and brake pedal, which will often scrape the rut walls.
- Keep toes pointed upward.

4. Dobb has successfully executed the turn and is focused on the next obstacle. Notice how his head is directly over the handlebar to keep the bike from wheelying. This is necessary because this particular rut was very tacky and traction was abundant.

Avoiding Ruts

In the same turn where James Dobb railed the line perfectly, Larry Ward has chosen a more aggressive approach. Ward has gone up on the banking, which is full of traction, and has opted to square off the turn and avoid the rut altogether. To safely accomplish this approach, Ward crosses the rut as perpendicularly as possible so the groove doesn't catch his front wheel. In essence, he's treating the rut like a small hole and simply allowing his suspension to absorb it as he accelerates aggressively to the next obstacle.

Deep Ruts

1. This is a classic example of a rutted corner. As you can see, there are lines all over the place. Even in this moderately deep rut, Steve Lamson is already scraping the chain guide against the inside rut wall, which makes cornering much more challenging.

2. Lamson gets on the gas harder as he approaches the exit of the corner and the front end starts to lift. Had he been mid-rut, his small wheelie might have forced his front wheel over the rut wall, which can easily cause a rider to crash.

Descending Ruts

Riding in a descending rut can be extremely tricky, especially one that comprises the exit of a turn. Typically, the front wheel wants to jump out of the line under acceleration. Normally this would entice the rider to add more weight to the front end of the bike, but not in this case. Too much weight on the front end could cause the rear wheel to lift out of its groove. Patience, liberal throttle application, and centered seat positioning are all qualities that work well in this situation, as James Dobb demonstrates.

Climbing a Rut Wall

Mike LaRocco's wheel has started to ride the outside of the rut wall and now wants to jump out of its line. This is an indication that the rider is trying to go too fast without leaning over enough. To settle the front end, LaRocco backed off the throttle and leaned further into the inside of the corner, which allowed the bike to make corrections.

Chapter 10

WHOOPS
Timing and Rhythm are Key

Whoops are one of the most challenging obstacles, period, and they are designed to be that way. In a nutshell, whoops are usually created to break up a rider's momentum to test skill, endurance, line selection, and motorcycle setup.

Because there are many types of whoops, there are few guidelines that riders use with any frequency. Some whoops require a double or triple jump technique to be used repeatedly, while others mandate a skimming approach for quicker navigation.

Body Position

The most important thing that will make you a better whoop rider is body position. In nearly every instance the idea is to stand up all the way through the whoop section. This will allow you to absorb some of the shock with your arms and legs. You'll need to shift your body position as you go through whoops, but your body should be a bit back of center most of the time. In deep, wide-spaced whoops, you typically want to skim the front tire from peak to peak. In this case, your body position will shift back a bit (but not so far that you are hanging out over the rear fender). When the whoops are more abrupt and tightly spaced, you typically will stay centered and let the front and rear of the bike soak up the impacts. The key here is to stay centered and let the bike rock back and forth when it hits a bump.

Try as many lines as possible in practice, and be prepared to adjust your lines during the race. Whoops typically change as the race progresses, and the fast line may move around. Also, whoops can be a good place to pass, as long as you take a different line than the rider in front of you. That way, you'll be poised to take advantage of any mistakes.

Heads Up!

The second most important aspect is to stay alert and keep at least a finger or two on the clutch and front brake in case you have to stop quickly. Pay attention at all times because whoop sections are very unpredictable. Never get too confident; otherwise, they may bite you.

Front Wheel High

Thirdly, most success is determined by the initial approach. Most, but not all, require riders to enter the whoop section with the front wheel high. The general idea is to keep the front end light so that it can skim over the top of shallow whoop sections. When using this skimming technique, it's important to

The attack position is usually the preferred riding position and is used as the basis for most whoop riding. Note that Danny Smith has shifted his weight back to keep the bike level. In most cases, the front wheel should be level with or above the rear wheel through the whoops.

Effective whoop riding requires the straightest shot possible at each successive whoop. This is the only way the suspension will be able to do its job effectively; otherwise, the rear end will tend to wander, which could eventually lead to major swapping.

Steve Lamson finds the fast line through a set of whoops. Note that although his weight is back, he's not hanging his butt over the rear fender (which would be too far back).

Avoid dropping the front wheel into the face of a whoop at high speeds. This is a recipe for disaster, even if you are talented and strong like Mike LaRocco. Fortunately, LaRocco recovers by shifting his weight to the back of the bike and extending his arms so they can act like shock absorbers upon impact.

keep your weight toward the back of the bike. Too much weight on the front wheel could cause the bike to stab a whoop and cause you to go over the handlebar.

The fourth tip is to work your way up to speed on each and every type of whoop you encounter. Riding too aggressively could land you on your head.

Doubling and Tripling

Aside from skimming-type whoops, you will most likely encounter whoops that are too far apart to skim, but close enough to double, triple or even quadruple jump. If so, resort to regular jumping techniques.

"On whoops that you're jumping instead of skimming, try not to overjump them when you are doubling," recommends Steve Lamson. "If you land on the face of another jump, your suspension may rebound you kind of weird and it may not toss you where you want to go. Your suspension will also get screwed up if you come up short or case it. The best way is usually the smoothest."

"If you're jumping the whoops, use your legs to get a little extra lift," Ron Lechien adds. "Before the first whoop, bend your knees to the point where you are almost sitting, and then push down really hard on the face of the jump, which will further compress the suspension. As you push down, your legs will straighten up momentarily, and then you will need to bend them quickly (once again) as the bike lifts off the ground. All of this has to happen in a split second to work."

"In practice, try as many lines and techniques as possible," Jeremy McGrath recommends. "This will give you a good feel in case you have to get out of your line to pass another rider."

"Usually ruts will develop one good line that everyone will use because it's an area where the whoops are getting worn down," insists Lamson. "Most of the time you should use that line, but always look for alternatives."

"Keep an eye on the whoops throughout your race," Mike Craig adds. "Sometimes a better line will develop as the race progresses."

WHOOPS

- Stand up so you can absorb the shock with your knees and so you can frequently redistribute body weight.
- Pick the straightest line possible.
- Look for the smoothest line.
- Pick a gear that will give you a quick burst of power when needed.
- Avoid following other riders.
- Stay off brakes unles absolutely necessary.
- Keep your front end light.

The only time your front wheel should be this high is if you're starting from a near dead stop. This way you can wheelie over a whoop or two to begin a good drive.

WHOOPS

Mastering whoops requires good body position and great timing. Most jumping techniques apply to whoops as well.

Because this row of whoops has a major gap at the beginning, John Dowd alters his style accordingly and prefers to double jump into the section. Here he's using an advanced sit-down approach, which will give him more lift as the shock rebounds quicker than the normal standing position. The maneuver is difficult because it also kicks the rear end up rather rapidly, which also causes the front wheel to drop suddenly.

Doubling Whoops

RELATED SECTIONS: ACCELERATION, JUMPS

#39 ROW THE BOAT

Time the rowing action of your body with the compression and rebound of bumps and other obstacles on the track. You need to row back as the rear wheel tries to kick up.

Many riders just ride the motorcycle across rough ground or whoops and never try to time how they weight and unweight the suspension. The result is that the motorcycle ends up weighting and unweighting their bodies with a mind of its own.

This technique requires good timing and anticipation. You have to anticipate where you're going to weight and unweight (to help the suspension compress and rebound) the motorcycle in

order to make it compress, skip, jump, fly, and land just how and where you want it to. This is not just a straight up and down movement. While you're helping the suspension compress down and rebound up, you have to move back and forth in order to keep the motorcycle somewhat level.

Learn to do this right, because I guarantee you, it will feel good and you'll live longer.

"The harder you work, the harder it is to surrender."

#40 THROTTLE LAUNCH

Use the clutch and throttle to launch you out of whoops, jumps, and certain kinds of bumps.

As we mentioned before, a common mistake is to use just the throttle

alone instead of the clutch and throttle together. To launch the bike with the throttle, you need precise timing of the power hit to the rear wheel. If you just use the throttle, you're not always going to be able to match the right amount of power and timing to the rear wheel.

In this case, the clutch is used more like a trigger. You want to trigger the clutch with the correct timing of the throttle as the bike compresses into the jump or whoop. This technique will give you better control of your launch and more height and distance.

Practice this carefully on larger, sharp-edged bumps or small tabletop or other safe jumps before trying it on big jumps.

"The first principle of success is desire, knowing what you want. Desire is the planting of your seed."

Skimming Whoops

1. This is a prime example of a manmade whoop section. The whoops are fairly close to one another and they are about 1 1/2 feet tall. Jeremy McGrath enters the whoop section while standing with his weight centered, and knees and elbows bent, but adds a little weight to the front end as he crests the top of the lead whoop. The weight added to the front end will help set him up so he can get the bike parallel to the ground, which is necessary to get the best drive while in this skimming-type whoop section.

2. McGrath quickly adjusts the attitude of the bike so that it's parallel to the ground. The idea is to skim across the top of the whoops (not allowing either wheel to dip down into the trough). This photo perfectly illustrates how McGrath strives to make contact with each and every whoop to maintain maximum drive.

3. Occasionally even the best riders in the world have to let one wheel or the other dip into a trough. When this happens, the idea is to rebuild momentum quickly, which usually requires double jumping the next whoop, landing on the downslope, and then readjusting body position to get the bike parallel to the ground.

4. This is the same obstacle on a different lap. McGrath gets the front end twisted and has to back off the throttle to avoid getting the bars ripped out of his hands, endoing, or both. Effective whoop riding always combines careful throttle control and clutch use while continually repositioning one's body.

Chapter 11

OFF-ROAD OBSTACLES

Nature's Way of Fighting Back

One of the joys (and pains) of riding off-road is obstacles. In motocross or even some hare scrambles and cross-country races, the obstacles tend to be ones that you see several times and work up to crossing at speed. Enduro and trail riders, on the other hand, typically encounter these gifts from Mother Nature unexpectedly and only a few times. Riders have to think quickly and learn to adapt their techniques to rapidly changing conditions and obstacles that loom around every corner. For this reason, off-road riding is a great way to improve your skills. It forces you to be creative and deal with situations quickly and efficiently.

For each of these obstacles—trees, rocks, water crossings, and so on—there are techniques that will help you deal with them speedily and in one piece.

Trees

Trees are one of the least-forgiving obstacles on the planet. In essence they are like tall, skinny rocks with arms, and are capable of causing great pain with a single, glancing blow.

Because trees can grow almost anywhere, their presence can make even the simplest obstacles far more treacherous. Hence, the rule of thumb is to avoid trees! Like an Akido master, they approach violence passively; if you don't hit them, they won't hurt you.

Sometimes the best way to go fast through trees is to go slow. You'll lose some time, but going slow is better than going fast

Many riders, like Ty Davis, cut down their handlebars so they can squeeze through trees much easier. As you can tell in this photo, many trails offer very little room to negotiate. This photo also illustrates why it's important to tuck in your elbows.

for a little while, crashing, and going fast some more until you crash again. Mistakes can be extremely time consuming, plus they waste lots of energy.

"Near trees I ride with my knees tucked in as close to the bike as possible to prevent my legs from getting hit," says Guy Cooper. "I also try to keep my toes pointed in so that they don't snag on anything."

"Pay close attention to width when you're splitting two trees," adds Cooper. "If you're not sure if you can safely make it through, then you should stop. If it's too narrow to attack at speed, usually you can push one end of the handlebar through at a time, kinda wiggling your way on by, and then continue."

On the same note, Scott Summers adds, "If you ever have to ride under a fallen

The shortest distance between two points is a straight line. When trees obscure the path, riders frequently try to get as close as possible to them only to discover the painful penalty for getting too close.

TREES

Guy Cooper—"I always cut my bars when I know that I'll encounter trees. Usually, they are less than 30 inches wide; however, this is one area where it's best to experiment to come up with your own width."

Scott Summers—"I wear forearm and elbow guards to protect myself from any contact."

Guy Cooper—"If your bike is water-cooled, make sure you have a good set of radiator guards that offer side protection. This is the best way to prevent damage in case you smack a tree."

Ty Davis—"I'll use a brake snake [a piece of cable run from the brake pedal to the frame] in the woods to keep the rear brake pedal from getting damaged."

Larry Roeseler—"I always like to use heavy-duty inner tubes when riding around tree roots because they can cause flats just as easily as rocks."

tree, make sure you have plenty of headroom. If there is any question in your mind, come to a complete stop for further inspection and then proceed. There may be broken branches or other things that could cause you injury."

It is fairly common for riders to underestimate their overall height when riding under trees. It is easy to forget that a helmet adds almost two inches, and some people fail to realize that even if they are ducking with their chin resting on the gas tank or seat, if they hit a tree, their head can't go down any farther. The result could injure the rider's head, neck, back, or all three.

Riders also tend to forget that their drink system, when used, adds a couple inches to their overall height when crouched over. It is not all that uncommon to see a rider get momentarily stuck because their drink system has caused them to get wedged between their bike and a fallen tree.

It is also extremely important to watch out for downed trees lying on the ground (see the upcoming section on log crossings). Noth-

Sturdy aluminum or plastic handguards are used by most woods riders to prevent hand injuries. Even low-speed collisions can break fingers, hands, wrists, arms, elbows, and other bones. Good handguards also prevent the levers from being bent or broken.

ing will send you over the handlebar quicker than hitting an immovable object.

Aside from tree trunks, there are several other items you have to avoid: branches and roots.

Because branches are usually found in shaded areas that can be very dark, it is very important that riders pay close attention to their surroundings at all times. "Watch out for tree branches that could knock you off your bike or jab you like a spear," says Cooper. "These can be as dangerous as the trees themselves, and they can be easily disguised."

And wherever there are trees, there are bound to be tree roots. Remember, the closer you are to a tree, the larger the root. Unfortunately, roots can also be easily camouflaged due to the lack of sunlight and surrounding foliage. Small bushes and leaves can give riders a false sense of security, but it only takes one encounter with roots for a rider to remember their painful potential.

Rocks

It's hard to imagine, but a 100-yard-long rock bed can be as damaging to both man and machine as a 100-mile section of normal

TREES

- **Watch out for roots that can be hidden under leaves.**
- **Keep an eye out for low branches that could knock you off your bike.**
- **When splitting two trees make sure there is enough room to safely negotiate.**
- **When riding under a fallen tree, make sure you have enough room to squeeze by, and remember that a helmet and drink system add height when in the crouched position.**

PRO SETUP TIPS
ROCKS

Guy Cooper—"Use as many guards as possible to prevent damage to your bike. The last thing you need is a rock breaking your center cases or bending your rear rotor."

Ty Davis—"When I know that it's going to be real rocky I will use a brake snake. A brake snake is a small cable that attaches from the brake pedal to the frame to prevent the brake pedal from being severely damaged if it were to encounter a rock."

Guy Cooper—"In rocky areas I always use a steering stabilizer. I also find steering stabilizers useful for high speeds and have even used them in outdoor motocross."

Ty Davis—"Most of the time I recommend using heavy-duty inner tubes even if you don't expect to encounter rocks. A flat tire will waste time on the trail."

Guy Cooper—"If it's really rocky I will use a bib mousse [a solid foam insert that replaces the inner tube] so that I'm 100 percent certain that I won't get a flat tire. That way you can ride as aggressively as you want without any fear of tire failure."

Larry Roeseler—"I use a shark fin to protect the rear rotor. The shark fin replaces the standard plastic rotor cover found on most bikes and is nearly impossible to bend."

Guy Cooper—"When riding in rocks, I use bark busters to protect the levers in case I fall. You don't waste time changing levers on the trail."

trail. In terms of composition, rocks are harder than normal terra firma, and therefore become more damaging, even when a crash occurs at low speed.

Rocks are difficult because they offer absolutely no give, unlike most terrain. Simply put, most suspension doesn't know how to react when it comes into contact with something that doesn't want to give, even a little bit. Take sand, for example. The general nature of sand is to absorb a lot of energy. That's why you can jump higher when you know you'll be landing in a surface that provides a cushioning effect.

Rocks, meanwhile, tend to force most forks to deflect rather than absorb the impact. This is why most professional riders will agree that the best approach when facing

rocks is to use finesse. Muscling your way through a rock bed is a sure-fire way to get yourself hurt.

In most instances, the best approach is to stand and carry your body weight slightly rear from center. This will unweight the front end slightly, which allows the suspension to work more effectively. The rearward weighting enables the front wheel and fork to bounce off obstacles without as much disruption than if more weight were placed on the front end.

"Try not to tense up when you're riding in rocks," Ty Davis recommends. "This is probably the most common problem, because most people are extremely fearful of crashing and therefore ride extremely rigid. Though it may seem difficult at first, allow the

bike to work beneath you. If you let them work, most bikes will do a decent job of riding over rocks."

Technique is also based on line choice. In general, it is much easier to travel straight through a rock bed than meander. Turning will only have a poor effect on the suspension and tires, which will make the task more challenging.

Typically, the best path is the shortest, but it all depends on rock size. In most cases you want to stay away from the larger rocks. They can be very damaging to both you and your bike. If you must ride near rocks that are footpeg-height or taller, Davis suggests to "ride with your toes facing upwards. You can't believe how many people break their feet and their toes by smacking into things they 'didn't see.'"

Rock shape is important, too. Sharp, jagged-edge rocks are very prone to cause flats, and round rocks are generally more slippery—you have to be the judge and predict how your bike will react. Wet rocks, though, are usually the worst, because traction is almost nonexistent.

Because traction is a prevailing problem, most rock specialists tend to avoid excess wheelspin and stay off the clutch. Instead, they let torque work them through a rock bed.

While standing is the preferred method, sitting can be an effective way of negotiating fairly even rock beds at slow speeds. Sitting can help provide traction to the rear wheel on inclines, plus it allows you to lift your feet off the footpegs to avoid rocks that have the potential to break your feet.

You do, however, have to be careful with foot placement. Both feet should be kept on the footpegs at all times unless you are forced to dab or miss a rock. Anytime you take a foot off the peg you generally lose some of your

Typically, it is best to approach a rock bed while standing up with your weight centered on the bike. The idea is to choose the smoothest line. Emphasis should also be placed on avoiding wheelspin, which will usually send the rear wheel into a pinball-like state. Once the rear wheel starts bouncing from side to side, it's extremely difficult to regain control.

It's important to stay on the lookout for rocks that may be hidden. This 250-pound boulder was covered in moss and nestled behind a leaf-covered branch. Nonetheless, it breaks everything it comes in contact with. Even small rocks at low speeds can break toes, smash pipes, bend brake pedals, and destroy engine cases.

ability to help the suspension soak up impact because your knees are almost useless unless used together.

Dabbing in rocks is also extremely dangerous because the only times you usually are forced to dab are in areas composed of large rocks. Large rocks make it more difficult to find a place to drop your foot because it is real easy for your foot to deflect off a rock at speed and cause it to go in a direction you don't want it to go. The results can be very painful and damaging to knees, among other things. However, if you pay close attention, you can survive.

ROCKS

- **Look for the smoothest line.**
- **Watch for bowling-ball size rocks that could hit your footpeg and injure your feet.**
- **Watch out for hidden rocks.**
- **Stay focused and avoid being overly aggressive.**
- **Avoid wheelspin.**
- **Make sure your bike is -protected with guards.**
- **Watch for sharp rocks that could cause flats.**
- **Try to keep your feet on the footpegs as much as possible.**

If there is a line that is smooth enough where you feel comfortable sitting down, you still have to remain alert. In this turn, Ty Davis has discovered that it is best to remain seated because it would be too difficult to lift his left leg over the rock while standing. Notice how Davis raises his leg as high as possible without interfering with the handlebar.

Water Crossings

Water crossings are one of the most mysterious elements in off-road riding because of the secrets that water hides beneath its surface. Rocks, tree roots, mud, sand, and even depth itself make water crossing extremely challenging most of the time.

The most important factor is evaluating the situation. First, you have to make sure that the body of water is, in fact, crossable, and that may not always be easy. This is where your own judgment will come into play. If you are unsure, try walking across, or simply look for an alternative line or turn back.

Another determining factor is current. If the water is moving swiftly, you could easily get knocked off your bike and put yourself in serious danger. Many riders underestimate the power of current. If you are concerned, don't try it.

PRO SETUP TIPS
WATER CROSSINGS

Ty Davis—"Make sure that your entire electrical system is sealed properly; otherwise, your engine could quit rather abruptly. When this happens, it will take you forever to get it started again."

Guy Cooper—"Use a good skid plate to protect your engine cases from rock damage."

Ty Davis—"Seal the airbox really tightly so that water can't get inside the engine. I usually take the entire airbox apart and seal all of the joints with silicone. If there are any holes on the side you should cover them up with duct tape."

Crossing Water

Before crossing any body of water always make sure you have a good idea of the depth. Though it's not always easy to gauge, strive for the shallowest point to make your crossing. Wheelying across can be a good way to keep dry, but keep in mind that the resistance of the water will pull down the front end. Also, you need to be certain that the bottom of the river is relatively smooth (a hidden log or rock could give you a quick trip over the bars and into the drink).

If you determine that the water is safe to cross, you should pick the shallowest, most direct route and proceed slowly so you don't splash water into your airbox. The best method is to stand with your weight centered so that you can be prepared in case you sink into a hole or the bike hits a rock or another hidden obstacle.

"If there are too many rocks, you may want to consider walking your bike across," suggests Tommy Norton. "This will reduce the risk of cutting a tire on underground rocks. You also have to watch out for underwater ruts in places that are used by a lot of riders."

If the crossing isn't too deep, Guy Cooper has a recommendation: "When I know the water is fairly shallow and doesn't have any rocks, I will sit on the seat and lift my legs as high up as possible to keep my boots from getting soaked. Moisture is one of the main causes of blistering, plus it's not a whole lot of fun riding in wet boots."

Cooper also has an answer for small crossings for really experienced riders. "If the stream is really narrow you may consider wheeling across. This will decrease water spray, which could spoil your goggles, plus you don't have to worry about hitting any hidden rocks that could cause your front end to twist."

Log Crossings

Fallen trees can be very intimidating, especially the large ones. Things such as ground clearance, traction, and gravity sometimes make it seem impossible to get over such an obstacle, period—let alone in total control. When there are no alternative lines to pursue, and you don't want to turn back, there are a couple techniques commonly used.

The most popular is the ultra-low-speed wheelie approach. This is where riders use careful throttle and clutch control to loft the front tire over the log, all the while making sure the rear end doesn't slam into the other

Getting over down trees is a tough but not impossible chore. When all else fails, it may be necessary to lift the bike over. The easiest method is to get the front wheel over first, then rest the bike on the lower frame rails, then lift the back end over.

Lowering the Front End

1. This is the exact same log, but Cooper is coming from the other direction to more clearly show how to lower the front end. This is a crucial moment because the front end must be lowered very quickly, but it's tricky because you still need power to drive the rear wheel over the log. Though careful throttle control is very effective, most riders prefer to slip the clutch momentarily, just long enough to drop the front wheel, and then let the clutch out so the rear can maintain momentum. At this point you want to avoid too much rear wheelspin that could cause the back of the bike to slide around on the face of the top of the log. When this occurs, maintaining control is extremely difficult.

2. As the front wheel touches down, the rear wheel should already be on top of the log. Notice how Cooper stretches out over the bike to make sure that most of his weight is over the rear fender. The added weight helps produce traction on the rear wheel, plus it helps prevent an endo from spoiling the technique.

Crossing Angled Logs

1. This log is much smaller, approximately 8 inches in diameter, yet it can still wreak havoc with suspension. The wheelie approach is used quite extensively on obstacles of this size; however, sometimes you may be forced to hit the log at an angle. In most cases this will cause the back end to slide out almost instantaneously and send the rider and bike crashing to the ground. One trick that riders commonly use is to find a V-shaped spot on the tree where you can firmly plant your rear wheel. This will make angled logs much easier to conquer.

2. Notice how Cooper's bike is almost perfectly parallel to the limb as he begins to execute this maneuver. As his rear wheel hits the log, his tire is instantly deflected by the branch, thus causing the bike to slide away from it.

3. As you can tell, Cooper's bike has maintained a straight line, thanks to the V-shaped crevice that used to be a tree branch.

4. As Cooper maintains a steady throttle, the rear wheel starts to spin and forces him to slide several feet down the log. This would normally cause a crash; however, a rider with Cooper's world-class balance is able to finesse through the section. Still, notice how the tire only gets on top of the log once it hits the V-shaped gap shown in the previous photo.

The most important factor lies with the terrain and conditions. It is absolutely, positively imperative that you don't exceed a safe speed; otherwise, you put yourself in serious jeopardy. In essence, you must always make sure that you have plenty of room to brake for upcoming obstacles. That means that you have to be looking far enough ahead so that you can see changes in the terrain. Never, ever assume something is safe just because it looks rather tame. Something as small as a one-inch deep rain rut can spell disaster if you are traveling at warp speeds.

You also have to be alert for two-way traffic. Even though you may have enough

Speed can be tons of fun, but it must be respected. A few simple modifications, such as attaching a steering stabilizer to the lower triple clamp, can make the bike more stable at warp nine. Sliding the forks lower in the triple clamps, which extends rake, can also help stabilize the bike.

Dealing with Speed

How fast is fast? To some riders, it's 40 miles an hour on a rutted straight on a motocross track, while to others, it's full throttle at 100 miles an hour down the Mexican peninsula in Baja. Regardless of the actual miles per hour, there are several tips that many top riders utilize when speeds get higher than normal.

PRO SETUP TIPS

DEALING WITH SPEED

Ty Davis—"Most riders will use a steering stabilizer when speeds get really high. It will take some of the nervousness out of the front end."

Guy Cooper—"One of the easiest ways to make your bike handle better at speed is to lower the fork in the triple clamp so that the top of the tubes are flush with the top of the clamp. This will extend the wheelbase, which should reduce headshake."

Ty Davis—"If you're racing, try to pre-run the course. This will give you a good chance to learn the area and also check gearing. If your bike is geared too low, you risk blowing up the engine, and you'll lose valuable time."

Flat terrain can produce incredibly high speeds, but it can also instill overconfidence. No matter how fast you're going, always be extremely alert and know your surroundings. *Joe Bonnello*

time to avoid fixed obstacles, don't forget about moving targets such as other riders or even the surrounding wildlife. Many off-road riders have run into animals; in fact, even motocrossers aren't immune. Multi-time World Champion Greg Albertyn hit a deer while racing a Grand Prix motocross race. It knocked him off his bike and nearly landed him in the hospital.

"Always be alert," insists Guy Cooper. "Most accidents happen when riders become overconfident."

At speed, it is also important to pay strict attention to body position. You generally want to weight the rear of the bike because this tends to reduce headshake while allowing the suspension to work more effectively. Most experts also insist on relaxing their grip on the handlebar so that the front end will be able to twitch naturally. Most riders find that if they are too tense, that they can actually induce a high-speed wobble.

If a high-speed wobble (also known as headshake) does occur, generally the rule of thumb is to get on the throttle as quickly as possible to help take a load off the front suspension. You can also lightly apply the rear brake. The worst thing you can do is slam on the front brake, which will worsen the headshake. Of course, if a dangerous obstacle lies ahead, you may have to take your chances, and get on the brakes as much as necessary.

Even if everything is going smoothly, it's always recommended that you keep your fingers on the clutch and brake levers and your foot next to the brake pedal at all times. This will speed up your reaction time in case you have to slow down rather abruptly.

Sidehills and Off-Cambers

Hills and mountains always pose many challenges, but one of the most unique involves off-cambers and the fine art known as sidehilling. This technique is used extensively for traveling across the face of the hill. When you find yourself staring at a gnarly grade that you have to cross, your sidehilling technique will be put to the test.

The trick with sidehilling is to avoid losing altitude. As you cross the hill, the slope and the force of gravity will make your bike tend to slide down the hill.

Another problem is finding traction. As with an off-camber, the sloped surface of the hill will leave the outside edge of your knobbies digging in air. With traction reduced, you are more likely to slide and less able to turn and accelerate.

Proper sidehilling always begins with a careful analysis of the situation. You must know exactly where you are going, and how you are going to get there. You have to look at the terrain type, keeping in mind that sand, snow, loose rock, and mud make it nearly impossible to sidehill, and look for other obstacles such as boulders, logs, tree branches, and anything else that may disrupt your travel.

If you can, stop and spend a little time planning a line before you tackle the sidehill. Choose an ideal line and pick some likely alternates to give you some options. Don't plan to fail, but if you see a particularly tough spot, have an escape route in mind if you get off-line. And don't try it if dire consequences lie below.

"Never try to cross over an area above a cliff," adds Ty Davis. "It's important to always have a path down the hill in case you can't make it all the way across."

When possible, look for pre-existing lines that travel across the face of the hill. These lines are very important, especially on extreme angles because they will help keep your wheels in line with one another. If you are going to cross virgin soil, you will spend most of the trip fighting the bike.

Ideally, you want to maintain as straight a path as possible, weight the outside footpeg for balance, maintain momentum without any sudden bursts of power, and make relatively few gear changes. Also, stay off the brakes because they will usually cause you to lose traction and start slipping down.

"If you have to brake it's usually better to use the rear," says Mike Healey. "If you grab a handful of front brake, the front wheel may wash out. That's why it's usually best to slow down by simply backing off the throttle and coasting to a stop. If you have to use the brakes, do so very carefully. Apply each one smoothly and slowly so you don't affect the handling."

Of the two wheels, the front is perhaps the most important, because it dictates where the bike is intended to go; plus, wherever the front wheel goes, the rear wheel usually follows.

Sidehilling can be done sitting or standing; in fact, sitting is usually the preferred method because it lowers the center of gravity. Then again, standing is sometimes necessary, especially if you approach an obstacle that will disrupt your suspension.

If there are not lines that you can use, and virgin terrain is your only option, you need to devote total concentration to your route. If the back wheel starts to slide, you need to add more weight to the outside footpeg. In some instances you may have to get on the throttle a little, but don't overdo it; otherwise, the bike will most likely dig in if the soil is soft.

If you are forced to cross sand, snow, or other loose terrain at an angle, you may have to allow the rear end to drop out of line with the front wheel. This technique will require more power than normal, but it is effective. Essentially, this is very similar to what pilots have to do to combat strong winds.

Regardless of terrain type, Bob Hannah insists that you should "always look far enough ahead so that you have time to change direction in case you see a rain rut or something else blocking your path."

"Pay attention to any changes in terrain that could affect traction," insists Ty Davis. "If you're going from hardpack to sand, you'll probably have to give the bike a little more gas to maintain your momentum. If the opposite occurs, and you go from sand to hardpack, you probably need to back off the throttle a little bit so that the wheel doesn't spin."

"If you're going downhill and decide that you want to sidehill across, the easiest way to get your bike lined up the direction you want is to brake-slide the rear end and then gently roll on the throttle once you get pointed in the right way," suggests Rick Sowma. "You need to be smooth, though. It will be difficult to slow down, because of the momentum, and you could highside once you get the bike totally sideways."

SIDEHILLING

- **Look for the smoothest line.**
- **Avoid excessive speed.**
- **Weight the outside footpeg.**
- **Make sure you know where the trail leads.**
- **Avoid sidehilling near cliffs.**
- **Look for the most traction.**
- **Use ruts or pre-existing lines to your advantage.**
- **Avoid sharp turns.**
- **Maintain momentum.**
- **Avoid quick bursts of power that will produce excessive wheelspin.**

Downhill 101

1. Downhills can be loads of fun when done correctly. Here, Guy Cooper displays proper body position: His weight is back near the seat/rear fender junction, arms are almost fully extended (though slightly bent), and he's gripping the chassis tightly with his legs.

2. This shot of Guy Cooper clearly shows the effect that downhill braking has on suspension. Notice that the fork is deep into the travel while the rear end is higher than normal.

"If you have to get off your bike because you can no longer keep going, it's best to get off on the high side," recommends Davis. "This will give you much more control over the bike and it will make sure the bike doesn't fall on top of you in case you have any big problems."

"Don't follow too close to other riders because if they have problems, you may have a difficult time getting around them," adds Healey, "especially if they are lying on the ground."

Downhills: Nature's Express Lane

Unlike uphills, where the challenge is making it to the top, the same can't be said about downhills and descending. One wrong move and both rider and bike will find that gravity offers an instant and unforgiving express lane to the bottom. That's precisely why most riders have a love/hate relationship with big descents.

When conditions are right, downhills can be a blast. But when terrain and/or weather turn nasty, downhills can be brutal and downright scary.

Most problems surround the difficulty to stop. Momentum is built quickly, depending on the severity of the angle, making it tough to reduce speed. Plus, downhills require careful body positioning and limited throttle use, which wreak havoc with suspension. That's because most suspension is set up to be balanced when your body weight is centered.

On downhills, the preferred body position is toward the back, yet the slope of the hill forces most of the (motorcycle and body) weight on the fork. Under braking, the fork will be bearing almost all of the weight. With the fork near the bottom of the stroke, you have very little travel available and the damping is harsh. Stutter bumps, hard braking, and an extreme downhill are a good recipe for an endo.

The best way to alleviate this effect is to accelerate, which takes some weight off the fork and puts it on the rear suspension. Under acceleration, your front end will rise a bit and be able to soak up rugged terrain much more effectively. Of course, you can't go down the entire length of most slopes at full throttle, so you want to accelerate hardest through the rough spots.

3. The use of the rear brake on downhills is vital and typically applied whenever the front brake is in use. Many riders also use the rear binders to brake-slide around turns. Notice how Guy Cooper's brake is activated with only slight pedal movement. Had the pedal been lower, it would be difficult to use effectively because of the body positioning required for riding downhill.

DOWNHILLS

- Never begin a descent unless you know you have a safe path to the bottom.
- Stand up with your weight toward the back of the seat.
- Avoid building too much speed.
- Watch out for bumps that could cause you to lose contact (i.e., traction) with the ground.
- Avoid grabbing too much front brake at once.

Downhills also toy with rear suspension, but in an entirely different manner. With most of the weight on the front fork, the rear end of the motorcycle becomes extremely light—which is why it's easy to endo. In essence, steep downhills actually unweight the rear suspension, therefore making the bike ride higher in the rear and brake action less effective. The result is that your rear brake has little or no stopping power and the rear end will kick up easily.

With your bike unbalanced, it becomes especially important that you pay attention to the terrain. In a lot of cases, you will occasionally have to accelerate hard over a bump, rock, hole, stump, log, tree branch, or what have you, just to get the front suspension to work properly. Although this is a rather aggressive approach, it's an effective technique.

Before you attempt a downhill, it's crucial that you have a safe plan mapped out in

your head. Motocross or other closed-course riders have the luxury of taking it slow a couple of times or even walking the hill beforehand (which is highly recommended). For off-road riders, downhills can be much more dangerous. It's not uncommon for riders to lead to a dead end where there is no safe, or rideable, way down. Things like rock outcroppings can trick you into thinking something is safe when it actually leads to a 150-foot vertical cliff with no way to turn around.

If you're riding in a new area, walking the downhill may be your best bet. And if you don't think you can make it, walking or "bull-dogging" the bike down is the safest route.

When traveling downhill, it is also wise not to follow another rider too closely or have a rider on your tail. If something happens to one of you, it could get ugly in a hurry.

Ruts add another nasty element to downhills. Ruts can be good when turning on sidehills, but make sure you don't get cross-rutted; otherwise, it will be difficult to regain control, especially if you are on a steep angle.

If you are worried about building too much speed and the effects of using the front brake, always remember that the rear brake will slow you down a bit. You can also use a technique that skiers use to descend, and that is traverse from side to side so that you drop at a slower rate. (See previous section on sidehilling for proper body positioning.)

Downhill Jumps

1. Even small descents like this mandate that rider weight be placed toward the rear of the bike. Although Ty Davis is jumping off the top, he still has to land on a downward angle. Though it looks as if Ty is sitting, he's actually standing in a crouched position and will remain standing until he reaches flat ground.

2. The theory behind most downhill jumps is to match the angle of the bike with the terrain. In this case, Davis has let the front drop down more than usual for a reason. He wants to get the front wheel on the ground as soon as possible to begin his braking.

3. Had Ty jumped front-wheel high, he would have risked the front wheel landing on flat ground. Notice that his front suspension has almost completely collapsed while his rear suspension is only halfway through the stroke. When transitioning from a downward angle to flat ground or an incline, it's usually advisable to back off the brakes to let the suspension absorb the impact.

4. As Ty reaches the bottom, he quickly, but smoothly, centers his body over the seat. Notice that the bike is balanced and that Davis is able to absorb some of the impact with his knees.

Furthermore, pay attention to the terrain and look for areas that will offer the most traction. Traction usually translates into control, which is essential when you are on the side of a steep incline.

If there's one thing to remember about downhills, it would be to take your time. It's difficult to emphasize how fast things happen while descending, but the penalties can be quick and severe.

Uphills and Cliff Climbs: A Higher Learning

Uphills are one of the only obstacles where technique alone won't always provide success. Though good technique is required for extremely steep terrain, the buzz word around hill climbs is usually power, and lots of it. Displacement pays off big, especially on steep grades, which is why big-bore bikes haven't slipped into extinction.

Cubic centimeters aren't, however, the only factor when it comes to success. Effective riding technique can make up for the lack of displacement.

Cliff climbs, on the other hand, also rely on power, but success is usually more dependent on technique, finesse, and confidence. In many ways, cliff climbs have a lot in common with uphills, but there are some very important differences.

Pick a Route

The first order of business is to examine the hill or the cliff. It's important that you look for an unobstructed route to the top. The idea is to avoid rocks, logs, tree branches, deep ruts, or anything else that could throw you off balance and rob you of momentum. When examining the situation, search for the easiest way to the top.

"Look for the straightest route up the hill and an area that is the least vertical," says Danny Hamel. "Most of the time it will be necessary to weave from side to side to follow preexisting lines, but always attempt the straightest shot possible . . . your tires will work more effectively."

Terrain is also important. Sand soaks up a lot of momentum and rocks tend to provide minimal traction. Along with mud and snow, all four of these elements will make your climb more difficult, at best.

Uphills are an incredible test of rider skill and machine capability. They can be extremely intimidating, but once overcome, they also reward riders with a sense of accomplishment.

Cliff climbs are very challenging because they usually require a series of quick rider movements combined with careful clutch use and throttle control.

Building Speed

Once you have chosen the best route, you should build as much momentum as you feel is necessary. You have to balance speed with impact and simple common sense. If the hill starts gradually, without an abrupt face, and is relatively open, you can hit it in a higher gear. If the hill has a sudden slope at the base, or is strewn with trees, rocks, ruts, or other obstacles, your attack speed will have to be lower.

In general, more speed is better. Remember, you will be putting more strain on your engine and it will be extremely difficult, but not impossible, to build more speed as you climb. Your only real option is to downshift as you go. On big-bore machines, you may not have to, but smaller bikes are likely to run out of beans as you climb.

Body Position and Traction

When you hit the base of the hill, it's important to stay loose and be in the attack position. As you climb, you'll need to move forward and backward to keep the rear wheel hooked up and the front end from wheeling. On most climbs, you'll need to adjust your body position to maintain traction. When the rear wheel breaks loose and spins, move your hips to the rear of the bike for more bite. If the bike wheelies, slide forward and lean over the bars to bring the front end down. If that isn't enough to stop the wheelie, slip the clutch to lower the front wheel rather than backing off the throttle.

Danny Hamel explains how he maintains good traction on uphills. "On hills that don't offer a lot of traction, it's good to sit as far back as possible to weight the rear end," Hamel says. "As traction becomes more available and causes the bike to wheelie, then you need to shift your weight further forward. You'll always find that you're constantly searching for the correct seat position."

Regardless, there isn't one right way; it all depends on the situation. In some instances you may find that you will have to sit and stand repeatedly while simultaneously shifting your weight back and forth to achieve the correct balance.

Take a Seat

On a smooth approach, you can attack the hill sitting down, as Ty Davis attests: "Un-less tackling an obstacle that will disrupt your suspension, usually you should be in the seated position, but exactly where depends on a lot of factors. The idea is to maintain traction by sitting over the rear wheel; however, this can cause the bike to wheelie.

"Most of the time the best body position for climbing steep hills is to be seated with your body weight forward to keep the bike from wheeling; it's basically the attack position. This way, if you need to stand for any reason, like to jump over a rain rut or hit a small jump, you can raise up pretty quickly and absorb a lot of the impact with your legs. On more gradual hills, sometimes standing is preferred, especially if there are a lot of acceleration bumps."

Smooth Power

Throughout the entire length of the uphill, power delivery must be smooth. For starters, it's important that you select the proper gear at the bottom that will put you in the meat of the powerband. In most situations it will be extremely difficult to upshift, so downshifting is your only true option.

You want to avoid excessive clutch work to build power. Every time you slip the clutch to build revs, you will most likely spin the tire and dig in, which can actually rob you of momentum. The clutch, however, can serve an effective role.

"On really steep uphills, if the bike starts to wheelie and you're already sitting as far forward as possible, you should slip the clutch a little instead of backing off the throttle," Hamel says. "If you back off the throttle too much it will be difficult to build rpm without a lot of clutch work. Whatever you do, you want to stay off the brakes unless absolutely necessary."

Bailing Out

If you do feel that you can't make it to the top of the hill, and there is no safe way to sidehill, it's usually best to back off the throttle, apply both brakes, and prepare to lean the bike over to one side. Some riders try to ride it out to the very end and believe that they have not given their best effort until they have looped their bike. After it's done cartwheeling 200 feet downhill, bending the bars, the radiators, both levers, and ruining the plastic, they realize that it may not have been the best approach.

Once you are forced to stop, try to get your bike perpendicular to the trail and step off the high side. Seldom do you ever want to have the bike above you on a hill because it's much more difficult to control, plus it is more likely to fall on you.

Cliff climbs are similar, but they are usually much shorter and based more on rider style.

"For cliff climbing it's usually best to stand up from start to finish," says Guy Cooper. "This will allow your body to absorb a lot of the shock that will occur as the bike goes vertical almost instantly. Sometimes the impact will cause the bike to bottom, almost like a G-out, and you need to be prepared.

"Watch out for rocks, tree roots, or anything else that could cause your wheels to deflect as you climb up any cliff because you can't afford to lose traction," adds Cooper. "Watch for ruts, too. They could knock your feet off the footpegs, which will kill your momentum. Remember, most cliffs are very unforgiving."

"Watch out for muddy cliff climbs, because you'll lose a lot of traction," Davis says. "Even the most basic cliff will become harder to conquer when it's slippery.

"Before you climb any cliff make sure you know what's on the other side. I've seen guys do some cliff jumps where they think the top is a plateau when it's actually a drop-off."

"Don't follow other riders up cliff jumps because if they screw up it will be almost

UPHILLS AND CLIFF CLIMBS

- Choose a route before attacking the climb.
- Maintain a steady throttle.
- Frequently adjust body weight to maintain traction without wheeling.
- Make sure you have selected the correct gear and, in most cases, avoid shifting.

G-Outs

1. G-outs occur when you are faced with a landing at the bottom of a jump or incline that bottoms out your suspension and hammers your body. Ty Davis shows how to handle the big hit. To most riders, this fourth-gear downhill poses an interesting dilemma because there's a drop-off at the bottom. Worse yet is the fact that the landing zone is a sand wash, which will rob loads of momentum upon impact. While some riders will instinctively brake hard to lessen the force of the landing, Davis decides to carry the front wheel high off the jump.

2. The impact bottoms Davis' rear suspension hard, but he's able to lessen the blow because the landing area allows him to stay on the throttle. The throttle continues the forward motion and helps his bike track straight in the sand. Fast deceleration in sand on this type of obstacle would normally be a tricky and dangerous feat.

impossible for you to make it to the top," adds Rick Sowma. "It's usually easier to make it to the top when you don't have to dodge the rider and cartwheeling bike.

"If you feel you're not going to successfully complete a cliff climb, it's usually best to jump off the bike to the side," Sowma continues. "This way your body should hit the face of the cliff and be able to use its traction to break your fall to the base of the cliff. You also want to get away from the bike so that it doesn't land on you or you don't land on it."

If and when you do make it to the top, you will have to lower the front end fairly quickly because the bike may be near vertical. The best way is to push down on the handlebar and add weight to the front of the bike. You don't want to go overboard; otherwise you could endo. It's also vital that you stay on the gas once you land so that you can power away from the cliff. Throttle application will also help your suspension absorb some of the impact.

G-Outs: Taking the Big Hit

Defined, a G-out is an extremely hard landing that bottoms the bike's suspension and jars the rider's body. In essence, it's a shock that generates enough G-force to exceed all the absorbing characteristics of the suspension components.

Though there are many ways to totally bottom a bike, a G-out is usually an obstacle where the forward motion is interrupted by an ultra-steep, or abrupt, incline. Sometimes this can include other obstacles such as a jump, water crossing, rain rut, or so on, but rarely are G-outs something that riders enjoy.

"G-outs are always tricky because you don't know the severity of the impact," Ty Davis says. "Always be cautious, and the first time you hit it, it's usually a good idea to go a little slower than normal so you know what effect it will have on your suspension."

Analysis is usually the most important part in taking on this obstacle. Because you already anticipate harsh bottoming, you should look for a location that is the least severe. Also watch for rocks, rain ruts, or weird variations in terrain that could further hamper your handling. Remember, since your suspension will most likely fully collapse, your engine cases will be lower to the ground and a rock could damage your cases even if you have a skid plate. Furthermore, your tires will fully compress and there's a good chance that when this happens in a rocky area you could get a flat and/or ding the rim.

Once you have committed, do all of your braking beforehand. If you slam into the other side with the brake on, it will only slow your momentum quicker.

In almost every instance, the preferred body position is standing, with your weight slightly rear of center. This allows your knees and elbows to help absorb the impact better.

It's also usually better to carry the front wheel a little high so that the shock can take the hit first and then transfer some of the remaining energy to the fork. To further reduce the harshness, it's fairly common for riders to give the bike gas to help maintain momentum.

G-OUTS

- **Adjust your body weight so it is slightly rear of center.**
- **Slowing down usually softens the impact.**
- **Keep your toes pointed up, so if you bottom, your feet won't get hung up on anything lying on the ground.**
- **Stand whenever you hit a G-out so your legs and arms soak up some of the impact.**

Rutted Hills

1. Rut riding is a skill that takes a lot of time to develop. Even world-class riders like Guy Cooper find that each new rut offers a multitude of new challenges. This line, for example, is blanketed with vines, tree roots, and downed branches. This is one of the rare cases where you may actually want to remove your feet from the footpegs, but only briefly.

Uphill Ruts: Momentum Is Your Best Friend

Riding uphill is difficult enough even when there are no ruts to worry about. A steep incline is a sure test of talent since proper body position, clutch use, and throttle control become critical factors in the quest for traction. If you lean too far forward there is a good chance you'll get wheelspin. The opposite extreme is leaning too far backwards where it's almost guaranteed the bike will wheelie and possibly loop out. You have to worry about all of this while dodging trees, rocks, and other obstacles.

The introduction of ruts drastically increases the difficulty of uphills, no matter how long or steep. They cause even the most experienced riders plenty of grief because it usually means that line choice is extremely limited.

In recreational riding and in racing, ruts form because of their popularity as the best or only line. In many cases, ruts will develop at the very bottom of single-track trails and/or any inside line, therefore affecting your momentum.

During most encounters with ruts you won't have many options. Though you can look for alternative lines on the outskirts of the trail, in most cases a better line will be hard to come by.

Just as in normal uphills, momentum is very critical. It's hard to accelerate quickly once you have begun your ascent. It's much more desirable to build speed before the hill because, in most cases, ruts will brush off more speed than they will help you generate.

You also have to remember that ruts are only as good as the people who make them. If the line wanders from side to side, it's because the original riders who dug the line had difficulty going straight. The same theory holds true for turns at the base of uphills. If the line is not smooth (perhaps it requires squaring off) then it's typically the first rider's fault, and so on.

Sometimes a single rut branches out into a series of ruts, which provides several options. Pay attention to what is happening up ahead so that you can make quick and instant decisions. If you don't like the way a line is working out, Ty Davis has some advice: "Look for a way out if you don't like where your rut is heading. Keep an eye out for a shallow point in the groove that leads to flat ground or a better line."

Furthermore, momentum is doubly important in ruts because contact with rut walls will brush off speed in most instances. On the other hand, you have to be careful about the opposite extreme.

"Riding too aggressively in ruts is not a good idea because it will force mistakes," says Ty Davis. "You want to flow with the bike as much as possible. Don't tense up, but instead, try to stay loose and fluid."

"Once you start going uphill, try to keep the throttle on as long as possible," adds Guy Cooper. "You lose speed quickly when traveling uphill and it's difficult to get it back. In most cases, I find it better to slip the clutch momentarily, to slow down, than to get out of the throttle. This way you'll be able to keep up engine rpm more effectively."

Ideally, you should enter the rut with both wheels perfectly lined up with the groove. If one wheel is slightly off there is a good chance that you will get cross rutted. When this happens it will be difficult to correct, and if you can get both wheels seated, you will probably have brushed off most of your momentum.

The terrain itself is very critical as well. Hardpack is usually good because excessive wheelspin won't deepen the rut that quickly, but it also doesn't offer that much traction.

2. At the base of this hill, Guy Cooper looks for an alternative line and finds it less than a half-foot from a group of ruts. In order to use the line, Cooper has to skirt to the extreme outside, but has found that his new line offers better drive to the awaiting uphill. As you can clearly see, Cooper's line offers him a straight shot, unlike the groove he's avoiding, which has a slight bend that would brush off speed.

Conversely, loam is great for traction, but ruts in soft dirt will deteriorate and will become unrideable rather quickly.

In most cases, it is usually preferred that you stay seated because it lowers your center of gravity. This is even more crucial when traveling uphill because you need to move forward and backward on the seat in the never-ending quest for the right amount of traction. (See previous sections on uphills and cliff climbs for more info.)

But when a rut becomes too deep, you may have to take your feet off the footpegs and start paddling. When trying this, it is very important to keep your weight as far forward as possible and have your feet near the footpegs in case you need to shift or stand on the rear brake.

Paddling can work, but it must be combined with proper throttle application and

3. One of the fundamental principles of hill climbing and rut riding is to keep your feet on the footpegs as much as possible. Any dab will cause you to lose momentum. Dabbing is usually the result of poor body position combined with a sudden handlebar correction. Typically, you want to keep your body weight centered over the bike. In this photo Cooper is leaning way to the side and his bike has started to wheelie. At this point he's got a whole lot of things to worry about because this is a good indication that he has lost almost all of his momentum. Before long he will have to start paddling with his feet in an effort to correct the situation.

UPHILL RUTS

- Line up both wheels before the entrance of the rut.
- Avoid wheelspin as much as possible.
- Too much clutch work could make your rear wheel dig in.
- Make sure the rut is not too deep.
- Don't follow other riders too closely.
- Maintain as much momentum as conditions permit.
- Watch for ruts that split into several lines.
- Make sure the rut exits in a desired location.
- Look for alternative lines.
- Watch for rocks, tree roots, or other obstacles protruding from rut walls.
- Avoid being overly aggressive.

4. This is an excellent aggressive approach by Guy Cooper. He's found good body positioning and appears to have plenty of momentum.

5. This line has gotten to the point where it is nearly unrideable. Notice that it's more than axle deep, causing the swingarm, axle, and footpegs to scrape against the rut walls, thus brushing off tons of momentum. At this point Cooper is simply trying to ride it out. In actuality he's unloaded all of his weight from the bike and is literally running with his legs. This puts less strain on the engine and doesn't force the bike deeper into the rut. Cooper's also trying to keep wheelspin to a minimum. Wheelspin will only succeed in making the rut deeper; therefore, constant attention must be paid to throttle and clutch control.

6. At this point the rear wheel is almost buried to the point where the rear sprocket will soon be underground. Cooper is nearly at the crest of the hill, so he's still taking a very aggressive approach. The depth of the rut forces Cooper to lean the bike from side to side in order to get any traction whatsoever. Also note that Guy is using his own strength to help muscle the bike to the top.

Trail Survival Tactics

Inevitably, you will have problems on the trail. It may be a simple mechanical failure, like a fouled spark plug, or you may find that you are trapped on the side of a hill. Either way, it's no fun and can spell disaster if you aren't prepared.

Fortunately, you are probably not the first to encounter these problems. There have been many unfortunate souls in the past who have had trailside problems, and you can benefit from the experience learned from these encounters. Here are some of the common problems and some of the most often-used solutions:

Getting Lost

If you become lost, seek high ground so you can search for reference points. If necessary, get off your bike and hike to the top of a hill or mountain whenever possible. Also, pay attention to the location of the sun—it is usually a good reference point. If you ride in an area that is popular, stop your bike and listen for other engines, which can give you an idea of where to head. More important, though, be prepared. Carry a compass and a map, if one is available. Take the time to figure out which direction to head if you get lost, and carry extra gas and water if you are in a vast, remote riding area. Lastly, use your head. If you lose your bearings, stop and survey the situation for a few minutes. Thinking things through is always preferable to charging off half-cocked.

Getting Separated

If you become separated from your group, don't ride off alone unless you are hurt or in danger. Remain in the location where you last saw other members of your party. In most cases, your buddies will backtrack to find you once they know you are missing.

Spare Tools

Unless you are riding on a motocross track, every member in your group should carry a fanny pack full of tools and spare parts. If you are in a large group, you may be able to consolidate, but spare tools and parts are absolutely mandatory.

Food and Drinks

Carry some type of liquid and energy bar with you at all times. Your body needs to be

weight distribution. Riders who get overzealous tend to overrev their bikes, which produces excessive wheelspin. In most scenarios, this is not a good thing. Wheelspin will just cause you to dig in to the point where your rear axle will get hung up on the rut walls and your tire will lose contact with the ground below.

If you do get stuck, try rocking your bike from side to side gently (you don't want to bend your rim), and then lift it out of the groove. The rocking motion will help free up the wheel from the rut.

fueled regularly; otherwise, it won't function properly. If you have to work hard on the trail, you'll be thankful you planned ahead.

Communications

Advances in technology have made cellular phones very inexpensive. If you are riding in a remote location you may consider packing a cell phone in case of an emergency.

Never Ride Alone

It is always recommended that you ride with another person. If you get stranded or hurt, that person may be the only person who can provide help.

Don't Panic

The most important item to remember in any situation is don't panic. Try to think rationally and try to determine what you could realistically do to get yourself out of a jam.

Trail Pace

If you do not feel comfortable with the trail pace set by other riders, slow down. If the group is large enough, the odds are that there is someone else who wants to go slower as well. Simply slow your pace and let the others wait for you. If this creates a problem, ask some of the other riders if they want to splinter off the main group and go on a less challenging ride.

SURVIVAL TIPS
- **Don't panic.**
- **Always ride with a friend.**
- **Carry a fanny pack containing spare parts and tools.**
- **Carry snacks and liquid.**

Turning Around

1. Just a few feet away from the top of this hill, Guy Cooper got stuck. The rut he was using became too deep and robbed him of all momentum. Though he was basically at the crest, Cooper decided that this was the ideal spot to show how to turn the bike around on a hill. It's a simple survival trick, but one you may use often when riding in hilly areas. "The first thing you want to do is get off your bike and keep it from rolling backwards," Cooper said. "Make sure that you stand on the side that is the safest and where you feel the most comfortable."

2. "Swing the back end of the motorcycle around by lifting on the fender," Cooper adds. "If you can't lift it all the way off the ground, then just slide it. "

3. "Bring the back end around until you sense that it will start rolling down the hill if you go any further," Cooper says. Notice the depth of the rut that Cooper's bike is straddling.

5. "While you're moving the bike around, pay attention to your footing," Cooper suggests. "The last thing you want to do is fall over while holding your bike."

4. "Grab onto the handlebar with both hands and begin rocking the bike back and forth, each time turning the bars to get the front end pointing downhill," Cooper instructs. "Continue rocking the bike until you have a straight path down the hill. It shouldn't take too long."

6. "As I prepare to remount the bike, I let the bike roll forward so I can swing my leg over the seat," Cooper says.

7. "With the brakes on, slowly get back on the bike," Cooper recommends.

8. "Only after you have yourself totally situated on the bike should you begin your descent," Cooper explains. "I rarely kickstart my bike . . . instead I bump start it on my way down."

Chapter 12

PASSING
Tricks of the Trade

Even if you get the holeshot, odds are that you will have to pass slower traffic at some point in the race. It's a difficult challenge at times, but it's not impossible.

The key is taking different lines than the rider in front of you. That way, if a rider bobbles, you can slip by him fairly easily. Another important aspect of passing is to use your head. Think about the pass a little bit, and it can save you a lot of trouble.

Where to Pass

A pass can take place anywhere on the track, but there are places where passing is easier. The most common is in corners, typically on the inside. By squaring off or simply taking a tighter line than the rider in front of you, you will be set up for a straight drive to the next corner.

Danny Carlson puts it simply: "One of the best ways to pass is to outbrake the competition and take their line away."

Done cleanly, you will get a better drive out of the corner and end up in front, as James Dobb describes: "One of the most common methods is to pass a rider on the inside of the turn. Go underneath the other rider and then out-accelerate them out of the turn. If they have a faster drive on the outside, then all you have to do is drift into their line so they have to back out of the throttle."

Block Passing

As Dobb mentioned, you sometimes need to take the other rider's line away to make the pass. This can be part of the end of the pass, when you are exiting the turn, or it can be a bit more deliberate. When you plan to take the rider's line away, it is known as block passing.

To do this, you have to be on the inside of the rider and turn so that you end up interfering with the rider's line. The rider will be forced to back off the throttle, and you can motor out front.

Done correctly, you'll give the rider enough room to see what you are doing and ample time to back off. Done incorrectly, you'll cut the guy off so hard that he can't stop and you'll both end up crashing.

Stuffing

When you block pass aggressively, it is known as stuffing. There is a fine line between block passing and stuffing a rider. You will see riders stuffing each other, to the point where they hit the other rider or even push the other rider off the track. On tight tracks or in other special cases, stuffing may be your only option, as Steve Lamson attests: "Depending on the track you're on, sometimes you may have to stuff a rider, especially if the rider is going about the same speed as you. You have to be on the inside

Consult with a friend or your mechanic (as Casey Johnson is doing here) to see if they have any ideas on good places to pass or ways to make up time. An observant eye on the sidelines can catch all kinds of helpful details that you can use in a race.

of the other guy and a little bit ahead of them so you can have less risk of falling and taking the other guy out, too."

Avoid following riders in the same line because you increase your chance of falling if they crash. It is also impossible to pass if you are in the same line all the time.

Passing on the Outside

Although the inside line is favored for passing, the outside can prove to be a good choice as well. The key here is raw speed. Mike Healey explains: "There are a lot of times where the fastest line will be around the outside of a turn, but people will take the inside so they don't get stuffed. If it looks like the other rider is committing to the inside then you may want to try the outside and try to slingshot around them."

You can also use an outside line to set up an inside drive. By coming in hard and wide, squaring the corner off deep, and coming back out with a good drive, you can make a solid pass. Danny Carlson favors this method on tight tracks, but with a note of caution: "When there are not a lot of lines available in the turns, I have found that going to the extreme outside of the corner and then cutting hard to the inside usually allows me to get a good drive to pass riders that are slower than me. The downside is that it uses a lot of energy."

Getting by on the Straights

Sometimes horsepower or a better drive can make the difference. If you can take a rider on a straight, the risk is minimal and the pass will be clean. Jeremy McGrath feels this is one of the simplest ways to pass, and it is a good way to pass lappers with minimal risk. "One of the easiest ways is to outaccelerate the other rider down a straightaway," McGrath says.

Passing in Whoops

Whoops are also good places to pass. If you can find a good alternate line in the whoops, you can often charge by a rider in front of you. Whoops are also places that riders tend to make mistakes, so be sure to take a different line than the rider in front of you in the whoops. If they bobble, you can pass easily.

Passing off Jumps

Jumps can be used to pass riders, especially if you have a fast line through a particular section. The tough thing about passing on jumps is that you can't change direction much once you are in the air. If you are going

Passing in Corners

1. The most common place to pass is in a corner. This sequence shows two riders (Mike Brown #26 and Damon Huffman #12) using different lines and coming out in nearly the same place. The classic pass move is to cut to the inside, as Huffman is doing. The other school of thought is to go wide and carry more speed through the corner, as Brown demonstrates.

2. At this point, both riders are side by side. Brown got a good drive off the previous corner and is carrying more speed, but Huffman's inside line is shorter and requires less speed.

3. It appears that the outside line looks to be the fastest because the rider, Mike Brown (26), has found a rut and is able to get on the throttle harder. Off-camber turns are extremely difficult because neither acceleration nor braking can be applied aggressively without the risk of losing traction instantly. Off-camber turns require finesse and excellent throttle and clutch control.

4. Remarkably, both riders are still dead even. Brown will need to corner smoothly and carry quite a bit of speed to make the pass, while Huffman will have to square off the corner perfectly and get on the gas as soon as possible. Whoever comes out on top, the rider in front has been made aware of the pressure. Making a pass stick may require several such attempts before you're successful, and just keeping the pressure on the rider in front of you can cause the rider to bobble, leaving the door wide open for you to pass.

OFF-ROAD RACING TIPS

Steve Hatch—"When you walk the track, look for alternative lines that you can use for passing. Know what spots are good ahead of time so that you can set up the other rider."

Ty Davis—"Rev your bike and yell at the guy to get out of your way. It won't always work but sometimes they'll move over or you'll make them nervous enough that they will make a mistake."

Danny Hamel—"Don't try to make a pass unless you're really sure that you're not going to crash. If you go down you'll waste a lot of time and may even get passed by other riders."

to try passing on a jump, be sure to choose an alternative line that gives the rider in front of you plenty of room. Larry Ward recommends, "Try different jump combinations to see if you can find anything that will give you the advantage even for a second. Once you're ahead, return to the normal race line."

When it comes right down to it, any place on the track can be good for passing. Stay out of the rider's line and be alert, and the pass may be handed to you on a platter. Steve Lamson favors opportunistic passing and recommends being patient and alert. "I think you have to pass them when you can, but sometimes you have to be patient because you can do something stupid and make mistakes. It's really bad to follow someone too long, so you need to take advantage of any opportunity that comes up," Lamson says.

5. As the pair enter the turn it could go either way. Damon Huffman (12), who has the inside, could take away Brown's line if he beats in to the turn and vice versa. Even though you don't get to see the end result, it demonstrates one of the fundamental rules of racing—when possible, don't follow the guy ahead of you. Passing is impossible when you're sharing the same line; plus, if the guy ahead of you falls, you risk getting taken out.

Preparation

Passing actually begins early in the day for closed-course riders. Walk the course and look for several good lines in corners, keeping passes in mind. Look for wide spots in the track, especially corners, and consider your strengths as a rider. If you are good in the whoops, spend plenty of time assessing alternative lines through the whoops. If you are good at squaring corners, look for sharp corners with an inside line you can use to dive under other riders. By the time you finish the walk, you should have three or four good places to pass in mind, with a bunch of other possibilities.

In practice, the same concepts should be applied. Try the lines you found in your walk as well as others, and adjust your plans accordingly. Riders are typically going slower,

so you can probably even practice passing in the spots you have picked out. By the time the gate drops, you'll have some ideas ready on where and how you are going to get around slower riders.

For riders who don't or are not allowed to know the course, where to pass will be determined by opportunity. In those cases, you have to be more creative and opportunistic. Guy Cooper recommends drag racing the guy: "Any time you get in a clear section of the course try to outaccelerate the other guy and then beat him to the next obstacle."

Passing with Pit Stops

Long races with pit stops can give you another opportunity to make a pass. "If the course is too tight and the rider you're trying

to pass is running almost your same pace, you may be able to pass them in the pits by getting in and out faster. This way you don't have to worry about making contact and risk crashing," Scott Summers says.

Think!

When making a pass, your brain can be your best friend. Before you go off half-cocked, stuff the guy, and end up off the track, think things through. First off, how much time do you have to make the pass? If you are a fast rider charging up from a bad start in a short moto, you need to pass quickly and take some chances you otherwise wouldn't. Don't be stupid about it (crashing will just send you back farther), but don't spend a lot of time stalking a rider. On the other hand, if you are in a two-hour-long hare scramble and are passing a rider who is just a bit slower than you are, it pays to stalk him for a while and wait for a good opportunity. Mike Craig prefers this technique for riders who tend to ride over their heads. "If you're trying to pass a guy who's kind of wild, then just wait for them to make a mistake if you can't normally pass them. Watch out, though. Don't wait too long because you may waste too much time and allow other guys to catch you," Craig says.

Applying Pressure

A good way to set up a pass is to show the rider a wheel, meaning you pull up close enough so the rider can see your front wheel. You may not be able to complete the pass, but the rider will know you are pressuring. This can sometimes cause the rider to tighten and make a mistake, leaving the door open for a pass.

In some cases, you can intimidate the rider into making a mistake, as Ron Lechien attests: "One of the oldest tricks is to scare the rider into making a mistake when they are braking. Pull up as close to the rider as you can, grab the clutch and then rev the bike really high so it startles the other rider. It even works better if you start yelling at the rider, too. You want to fool them into thinking that you're out of control and are going to run into them. They will usually panic and move over."

Attack, Attack, PASS

If the rider doesn't make a mistake, you have to determine a place to make a pass. If you are on a motocross track, you should al-ready have some ideas of where to pass. This is when you need to follow the rider and watch for your opportunity. "Always stay alert and look for any type of line that could help you make a pass. Every rider has their strengths and weaknesses and their weakness may be your strength," Danny Hamel says.

Be aggressive but do your best to avoid contact or taking the other rider out. The issue is not really sportsmanship or any other high-er moral ground, but practicality. If you have to collide with the other rider to pass, you can easily end up on the ground, which is the shortest route to the back of the pack.

In most cases, you'll have to show the rider a wheel several times before you can make the pass stick. As you follow the rider, watch his or her lines and try to figure out when and where there is room for a pass. "Look for alternative lines, maybe places that are the other rider's weak points. That's al-ways the best point for me to pass," says Steve Lamson.

Lamson also favors S-curves to set rid-ers up and knock them off. "Take advantage of S-turns because they're a good place to set up other riders. You can square the first part of the turn and then be set up for the next turn and make your pass."

In most cases, a pass is a series of well-calculated moves. Show the rider in front of you a wheel, follow until you have a good idea of some places you can pass, and then at-tack. You may have to set the rider up by sim-ply getting inside or side-by-side through one corner and finishing off the pass in the next. In some cases, it may take a series of three or four corners to finish off the pass.

> # PASSING
> - **Avoid following riders in the same line.**
> - **Look for places to pass during practice.**
> - **Don't try to pass a rider who is riding out of their head. Wait for them to make a mistake or crash, then seize the opportunity.**
> - **Outaccelerate the other rider.**
> - **Outbrake the other rider.**
> - **Off-road riders can pass riders through faster pit stops.**

"Sometimes you will have to set up for a pass a couple turns ahead . . . this is where knowing the race track pays off. Sometimes there's a good line out of a corner, but it's dif-ficult to get to at your normal speed. Well, when you're being slowed down by another rider you may be able to use that line," says Ron Lechien.

Lastly, if you find yourself spending every race passing people, you may have a different problem, as Danny Carlson explains, "If you constantly find yourself behind slower riders, it may be telling you something . . . you need to work on your starts!"

Chapter 13

What To Do When the Gate Drops

S T A R T S

Many riders will tell you that the start is the single most important aspect of any race, and the reasons should be rather obvious. Riders at the front of the pack can concentrate on riding their own lines, while those at the back of the pack have to contend with many factors such as roost, mud, dust, and slower traffic. Fast lines are hard to come by when you're stuck in the back of the pack, plus you expend more energy when you're forced to use those harder-to-get-to alternative lines.

Gate Selection

Most of the time the preferred starting spots are in the middle. Ideally you want the shortest, straightest shot to the first turn. Typically, riders starting on the extreme inside or outside get penalized more if they don't get a good drive into the first turn. They may find themselves getting pinched off in the corner and then getting passed up by the rest of the field.

On certain starting lines, the outside or inside may be a good line, although they are typically a bit riskier. An outside line can work if you can carry a lot of speed through the corner and come around the pack to the front. The disadvantage is that you could easily find someone in your line and have to brake and lose all your speed, putting you mid-pack at best.

An inside line can work if you can dive under the pack and square the turn. Here

A good start begins with gate selection and prep. Take this procedure very seriously and get to the staging area ahead of your competition.

again, you can easily get caught in a pile-up or simply be slowed down by other riders also diving to the inside.

The key to determining a good line is to watch the gate several races before your moto and see what gate positions seem to produce the most holeshots. More likely than not, you'll find that a bit to the inside or outside of center produces the best results.

Also, be sure to have several gate positions in mind in case you draw poorly and all of the spots you planned to use are filled.

Start Procedure

While you're in staging, pay close attention to the start procedure. Watch the

starter(s) and look for anything that could help you get a better idea of when they intend to drop the gate. At some tracks they let the gate fall at the same time every race, while other tracks tend to mix it up a little so that riders can't time the gate and get a premature jump.

Gate Prep

Once you've chosen the gate, you need to prep your starting gate. First off, look at your intended route to the first turn and then decide the angle of your bike. In most cases your bike will be perpendicular to the starting gate; however, at some tracks it may be necessary to angle your bike slightly. Regardless

Repeated practice is the best way to improve starts. Even if you feel confident, always take a few test starts during practice to see how well your bike hooks up.

PRO RIDING TIPS
STARTS

Greg Albertyn—"Try to stay calm. My best starts always come when I'm most relaxed."

Steve Lamson—"Concrete starting pads require totally different prep than normal dirt starting gates. On concrete the idea is to heat up your tire before the start of the race, just like drag racers do. This will help you get really good traction. To do this right I always have my mechanic clean the concrete with a broom so I can get more traction. Then, about 15 to 20 seconds before the gate's supposed to drop, I put my bike in gear, grab onto the front brake, stand on the tips of my toes (to unload the bike), and then spin the rear tire to get it hot and sticky. After that, I focus on the pin and get ready to start just like normal."

Ron Lechien—"Way before you go to the line, you have to have some sort of a plan. It starts with getting the best possible spot on the gate and then leads through to the end of the moto. When I know I'm racing against a lot of fast guys, it's important to get a good start and get to the front of the pack as soon as possible. When there aren't a lot of fast guys, then you can take your time and ride at your own pace."

Danny Carlson—"Pay attention to where the other riders are on the starting gate so that you know what to expect. If you know enough history about the riders you're racing against, then you'll know who may come underneath you in the first turn and try to take you out, and which riders may be intimidated by you."

Guy Cooper—"Regardless of what type of race you're racing, you want to get the best start possible. This will help you concentrate on riding faster rather than thinking about having to make up for lost time."

Steve Lamson—"Don't let other riders psych you out. Mental games play a part in every race, but try not to get caught up in them. If there is some psyching going on, you'd better be the one doing it."

A shovel and broom are two essential tools for good gate prep, and at most tracks, riders have to supply their own.

with any good start is total concentration and lightning-quick reflexes.

Gear Selection

Most riders tend to find that first is too low; therefore, second is usually the preferred gear. The best way to determine what works best for your bike is to practice starts before you get to the race. Some open bikes, in fact, work best in third gear.

Throttle Control

Getting the rear tire hooked up is key to jumping out to the lead. To do that, you need to have good throttle control. In general, you should use no more than half throttle until you clear the gate, then roll the throttle open. Also, watch out that you don't start over-revving the bike. Most riders tend to raise rpm without knowing it as they wait for the gate to drop. If you just rev the bike up and dump the clutch, you'll get too much wheelspin and be left behind.

Keep conditions in mind as well. On moist, loamy soil, you'll get good traction and can use more throttle on your launch. On concrete pads, traction will be hard to find and you'll have to use less throttle until the tire clears the pad and bites into the ground.

of the angle, make sure your starting surface is smooth and doesn't have any holes. If the actual gate is higher than your starting pad, take a shovel and try to raise the level of the dirt. If you start in a hole your bike will want to wheelie much easier, plus the bike has to work a lot harder to accelerate. Also, some tracks allow you to prep your line in front of the starting gate. If so, brush off the top layer

of soil with the side of your foot so you can get to the harder stuff that provides better traction. Also, toss aside any rocks, mud clods, or other debris that could disrupt your drive.

Mental Preparation

On the starting grid, most riders try to visualize the perfect start in their head. The key

When you watch the starts, before your race, keep an eye on how riders tires are hooking up. This can give you some clues on how much traction is available.

Use of the Front Brake

To make sure that you don't roll into the gate as you find the sweet spot on the clutch, pull in the front brake with your index finger and then let go of it the moment the gate drops.

Clutch Engagement

To speed up your reaction time, find the sweet spot on the clutch. This is the point where the clutch is pulled in just enough to keep the bike from moving. Then, once the gate drops, feed the clutch out slowly to avoid rear wheelspin.

If your bike wheelies, the clutch can be used to drop the front end, but otherwise you should use the clutch only for shifting until you get to the first corner.

Body Position

Lean as far forward as possible. Ideally, both feet should be on the ground, back arched slightly, head over the handlebar, elbows up, and eyes focused on the starting pin. The idea is to hold that position until you make a shift.

Once you are out of the gate, lean your upper body back to increase rear wheel traction and forward to let the tire slip a bit or bring down a wheelie.

Watch the Mechanism

Most tracks use backward-falling starting gates that penalize a rider who tries to get an early start. The gate essentially traps the front wheel, thereby forcing the rider to pull their bike out of its grasp before rejoining the pack. Most gates operate off a cam-type mechanism and have individual pins that hold the physical gate in the upright position. The pins are the first indication that

This photo shows the starting pin that holds the gate up. It's the first indication that the gate is in the process of being dropped.

On the starting grid take a good, long look at the line you intend to take to the first turn. Look for any large rocks, mud holes, or other things that could foul up your drive.

1. Three-time AMA 125cc National Motocross Champion Ricky Carmichael is one of the best starters of all time. He usually arrives at the gate very early and then tries to visualize the perfect start in his head.

STARTS

- **Get to the gate early for best selection.**
- **Visualize your entire start, including line choice and braking into the first turn.**
- **Get familiar with the start procedure before your race.**
- **Prep your gate for a smooth launch.**
- **Stay focused.**
- **Maintain steady throttle control, avoid overrev.**
- **Minimize wheelspin.**
- **Use the front brake to avoid rolling into the gate.**
- **Pay attention to clutch engagement.**
- **Select the proper gear.**
- **Lean forward.**
- **Watch the mechanism.**
- **Pay careful attention to upshifting.**

the gate is in the process of being dropped; therefore, 10 seconds before the gate's supposed to fall, watch the pin with total concentration and then execute your start once you see it move.

Shifting

You must concentrate on your shifting while racing down the start straight. One missed shift and the pack will leave you in their roost. Make sure that when you practice starts, you pay close attention to how your bike reacts during gear changes. For maximum power to the ground, shift the bike with the throttle wide open and without using the clutch. Some bikes require that the clutch be pulled in or the throttle chopped momentarily to shift.

2. Even though Carmichael's mechanic has already cleaned the concrete launch pad, he repeats the process to wipe away dirt that fell down once the bike was rolled into position.

3. This sequence clearly shows how important traction is to a good start. On concrete surfaces, most riders tend to overrev their bikes and get too much wheelspin once the gate drops. Generally, the tendency is to get impatient and forget about things like clutch control and throttle positioning.

4. Notice that Carmichael starts with both feet on the ground. This is something that helps him keep his balance out of the blocks. The most effective starting technique requires a perfectly straight line, and excessive body language is usually unwanted.

5. You can already see that Carmichael has a distinct advantage even though this trio has only traveled two feet. The goal of most riders is to stretch their initial gear choice until their elbows and shoulders are ahead of the flanking riders. If you throw a shift too early and you are the one with your shoulders caught behind, you'll generally lose the drag race to the first turn.

6. This photo shows how wheelspin has negatively affected Casey Johnson's (16) start. Notice that you can see the tread pattern on Carmichael's and Stephane Roncada's (22) rear tires, but Johnson's is just a blur. Johnson has also shifted his body weight to the right and is trying to compensate for the loss of traction. Remember, wheelspin will also cause a bike to slide sideways out of the launching pad.

7. Notice that Carmichael has slowly returned his left foot to the peg by drawing it straight up. He's ready to make his first shift and has already started to increase engine rpm.

8. Carmichael has done everything right and is already a full foot ahead of the other riders in this picture. RC was rewarded with a holeshot, one of the many he earned during the 1999 season.

Gary Semics' Absolute Techniques

STARTS

All the other techniques apply to starts, but here's some specially for starts. There are two races in each moto: from the starting gate around the first turn, and from the first turn to the checked flag. If you lose the race to the first turn, you are going to have to work that much harder to win the race.

Starting Technique

1. This sequence follows one of Mike Healey's (61) starts. Notice that his body weight is way over the front of the bike, his elbows are up, both feet are on the ground, and his eyes are totally focused on the starting mechanism.

RELATED SECTIONS: BODY POSITION
ACCELERATION

#41 SIT UP FRONT

Sit on the front part of the seat with your head over the handlebar clamps.

It's pretty obvious that you need to sit on the front part of the seat in order to pull a good holeshot, but I've seen riders sitting on the middle of the seat and not even know it. This makes it impossible to get your weight far enough forward to keep the front end down when there is good traction.

When you sit on the front of the seat, your weight is at the center of the motorcycle, right over the motorcycle's pivot point. As you launch off the line and down the front straight, stay in the front of the seat and transfer weight by leaning forward or back.

When it comes to starts, start off on the front part of the seat and stay there until you exit the first turn.

Concentration: "It is a process of diverting one's scattered forces into one powerful channel."

—James Allen

#42 MOVE FORWARD FOR TRACTION

Lean your upper body backward to increase rear wheel traction, and lean forward to keep the front wheel down.

When a nervous novice starts, he usually leans forward and freezes there, no matter what the traction conditions are like.

You need to be aware of what kind of traction you're going to get. This way you'll know how much you should lean forward, stay in the middle, or even lean back if it's really slippery (like on a

2. Once the gate drops, Healey smoothly releases the clutch, trying to find the optimum amount of traction during this drag race to the first turn. Move your upper body side to side to keep the bike straight and on line.

3. As the pack enters the first turn, Healey holds his outside line, which allows him to stay on the throttle longer than the riders near the inside line. While the riders on the inside of the line have to brake momentarily for the approaching right-hand turn, Healey's outside line doesn't force him to make as hard of a turn.

smooth cement start). Adjust your weight according to traction.

"The jack of all trades seldom is good at any. Concentrate all of your efforts on one definite chief aim."
—Napoleon Hill

#43 TWO FEET DOWN

Start with both feet down in front of the footpegs until you need to shift. Put your feet back on the footpegs when you need to upshift.

There are a lot of mistakes that riders make with their feet during starts. Some of the most common ones are:

- *Starting off with their feet to the outsides of the footpegs (feet can easily move back under acceleration).*
- *Starting off with their feet in back of the footpegs (the rider's feet will end up behind them. When a rider's feet go behind the pegs, the result is poor balance, too much weight behind the pivot point, and an inability to shift to the next gear on time).*
- *Trying to put their feet back on the footpegs as soon as they start to move (don't maintain good balance).*

By keeping your feet down in front of the footpegs, your feet will stay there throughout your start. This gives you better balance, keeps your overall body weight more forward, and leaves you in a good position to shift to the next gear when you need to.

When you want to shift, pull your left leg up and hit the shifter with the top of your boot as you put your foot back on the footpeg. It may take a little practice, but once you get it down, it's the best way to go out of the gate.

"You cannot have the success without the failures."

4. As you can tell, the riders on the inside have to cut the corner sharper than Healey.

#44 RELEASE THE CLUTCH SMOOTHLY

Feed the power to the rear wheel with the clutch and throttle as quickly and smoothly as possible.

The most common mistakes here are to dump the clutch too quickly or to slip it too long.

In order to get a good start, it's necessary to be quick, but at the same time you have to be smooth and precise with your clutch control. About the only place you can just dump the clutch and gas it is in the deep sand; other-wise, you have to feed the power to the rear wheel with the clutch and throttle together. This means you have to open the throttle and let the clutch out ac-cording to traction.

Be like a gunfighter on the start: relaxed, smooth, and lightning fast.

"What I do is prepare myself until I know I can do what I have to do."
—Joe Namath

#45 MOVE THAT BODY

Move your upper body from side to side to keep the motorcycle upright and tracking straight dur-ing the start.

Some riders freeze into one body position when they come out of the gate and just stay in that position. Or they drop their elbows and twist their upper body to try to keep the motor-cycle from veering over out of the gate. They don't have total control be-cause they fail to move correctly as things change.

5. At this point Healey is fourth, but by the second turn, his wide outside line that allowed him to carry more momentum, moved him up several positions.

An important movement to maintain this control out of the gate is side-to-side upper body movement. Start off with a lot of overgrip so your elbows can remain fairly high. From this position you can move your shoulders back and forth, parallel to the handlebars in order to keep the motorcycle straight out of the gate. To get used to the proper movement, practice this in a stationary position.

"He that would be superior to external influences must first become superior to his own passions."
—Samuel Johnson

Chapter 14

PRACTICE
The Only Road to the Top

The most vital part of riding technique is good body position, and the only way to develop better body position is to practice. The importance of these two facets of riding cannot be overstated.

Professional riders got to the level they are by hours and hours of practice. Talent, conditioning, and desire are all a part of excelling in off-road riding, but those three things are not enough. You have to practice.

Keep in mind that practice doesn't have to be grueling and repetitive, especially for amateur riders (most of us). Go out and try different things. Trail ride and explore side trails, climb banks and hills, or practice broadsliding down fire roads. Even within a small riding area, there are always new challenges. Experimentation is one of the most entertaining things to do with your bike, and is also one of the best ways to learn.

Learning body position isn't always fun and it isn't always natural. The key is practicing the correct body position until it becomes natural. Once you have that, everything else will come easier.

Improving your riding skills is not always an easy task. Though the learning curve is quite steep for beginning riders, it gets progressively tougher with time. There are, however, several steps that you can take regardless of your current ability. Keep in mind that the only way you are going to improve is through practice.

Take the time to set up your bike properly. The world is full of suspension companies who can help you get your bike dialed in if you don't feel confident doing it yourself. If your bike is not set up correctly you will never be able to reach your full potential, plus you risk personal safety. Guy Cooper demonstrates setting sag in his garage. Note that his feet should not be touching the ground to properly set race sag.

Static Drills

A basic place to start learning new skills is with the bike on the stand. Climb aboard and put yourself in the proper body position. Go step by step, making sure your elbows and head are up, you are overgripping the throttle, your feet are centered on the pegs, you have one finger on the clutch and brake levers, and that your head is over the handlebar mount.

Though it may appear rather obvious, the single most important ingredient to improved skill is practice. The more time you spend in the saddle, the more comfortable you will become. Here, Scott Plessinger rides in Illinois, where he has miles and miles of trails and tracks on which to practice.

To become well-rounded, try to ride in as many types of terrain as possible. In essence, don't limit your riding to one track or one riding area; explore them all. This is one of the most important aspects of improving, plus it should give you more confidence.

Have a friend videotape you in action. This way you can see for yourself what you are doing right and wrong, and you can watch it over and over again. This is one of the best ways to break bad habits, because sometimes you may think you are doing something one way when, in fact, you are doing it in a totally different way.

Once you are in the proper body position, practice sitting, standing, and shifting your weight forward and back in both positions. Pay close attention to where your body is when you move. You'll probably find that you will slip out of position once in a while, and can correct. This whole drill takes only a few minutes and, if you do it regularly, it can really help you improve body position. You can do it on a rainy day, after you adjust the chain, or just when you've got the itch to ride but can't get out to do so.

Challenging Terrain

When it comes to riding, one of the best ways to practice is to try different types of terrain. Try a new riding area. Go trail riding for the day. A day spent jumping logs, crossing streams, and tackling gnarly hills is a great

way for a motocross rider to improve, and a day at the track can be a great outing for an enduro rider. The broader your horizons, the more comfortable and skilled you will become.

Try a little trials-style riding. Ride along at a walking pace and hop over logs, big rocks, or short embankments. Keep your body in the proper position, and use the engine's low-end power and controlled bursts to tackle obstacles. This is both a good practice technique and a good way to warm up. (Hopping on your bike and immediately reeling off fast laps is a good way to pull muscles and increase the likelihood of injury; a few minutes of warm-up will save you a lot of pain.)

Wheelies and Stoppies

Wheelies and stoppies are also good practice techniques. Slow wheelies, where

you use balance and engine torque to ride a walking-pace wheelie, are especially good for learning throttle control, balance, and body position. The key is to keep your foot on the rear brake and hit it if you start to loop out.

Stoppies are done by sitting in a normal or slightly forward body position and braking hard enough to raise the rear wheel off the ground. Start small, at low speeds with gradual brake applications. Keep your elbows bent and your body loose and relaxed. If the rear end comes up too high, simply release the front brake.

As a variation, place your weight back and practice locking up the front wheel rather than doing a stoppie. Again, start practicing at a walking pace and work up to higher speeds. These slow practice techniques are a good way to become more familiar with how your bike will react to different situations. They

If you race motocross, spend a portion of each riding session pounding laps. Practice for a set amount of time, like 10, 15, 20, or 30 minutes, to simulate racing. When possible, ask a friend to check your lap times and keep track of them in some type of notebook. If they get progressively slower, there is a good chance you need to work on your conditioning.

are also a great way just to goof around and have fun on your bike.

Pounding Out Laps

Motocross riders should spend some time just pounding out laps. Pick a set number of laps and run those as hard as you can. This can be a good time to focus on a particular technique, especially the basics. Late in the moto is when your technique is most likely to sag, so concentrate on keeping your body in the right position as you get tired.

Also, don't mindlessly pound out laps. Pick a technique of the day, and work on it for a bunch of laps. For example, spend one day working on nothing but keeping your outside elbow high in corners. On another day, concentrate on braking technique. On another, work on using the clutch to get a smooth drive. You'll want to cut some laps just letting it all hang out, putting all of your skills together, but you need to focus on specific techniques to improve.

Outside Help

Have a buddy watch you ride and critique your riding. Explain to him what you should be doing. Better yet, show him photos from the book that demonstrate proper riding technique. Then, have him watch you ride and give you some feedback. Are your elbows high? Is your head up? Are you staying forward on the bike?

Videotape is also an extremely useful tool. As they say, seeing is believing. No matter what level your riding skills, you'll see something and want to change it. You also may be shocked to find you are doing things exactly opposite of the way you thought.

Riding Schools

One of the best ways to improve your riding is to attend a riding school. There are a number of these listed in the appendix, and all of these folks can give you some valuable feedback on your riding and tips and techniques that will make you a faster, smoother rider. Plus, riding school can be a good time.

Have Fun

No matter where you ride, do some play riding. This sport is fun, remember? Ride a wheelie. Try setting up for a corner in the air. Do some long power slides. Stay loose and

Motocross and off-road riders alike should spend a portion of their daily routine play riding. Practice throwing the bike around off jumps, learn how to wheelie and things of similar nature. Try some of these moves at slower than normal speeds to learn better balance, like Danny Carlson is doing here (you may even consider trials-type riding on your normal machine). Also, go trail riding every once in a while. Multi-time Supercross champ Jeremy McGrath is proof that play riding pays big dividends. "It's the best way to get familiar with your bike," McGrath claims. "It gives you a good feeling of how the bike will react if you get sideways or if the front wheel is too high or too low."

have a good time. Anything you do on the bike that is fun is good practice. Even if you're training to be the next Jeremy McGrath, don't forget to be loose and enjoy riding.

Take your time. This applies both to practice and racing. Many riders press just a little too hard and go slower because of it. If you slow down just a bit, you'll be able to see the track better and find yourself speeding up. Practice is the best time to do this.

Watch faster riders. What are they doing differently? What lines are they taking? This can range from watching the pros on television or at a race, to checking out the local A riders. Also, if you get a chance to ride with faster riders, don't pass it up. Follow them and learn (but be careful not to get sucked into trying something above your ability).

All these techniques aside, the single most important thing is simply to ride as much as you can. The more you ride, the better you'll be. If you spend some of your riding time concentrating on improving, you'll get better more rapidly, but riding makes you a better rider. It's that simple.

Above: Following faster riders is a good way to figure out faster lines on a track. Pay close attention to their body position, brake markers, acceleration points, engine rpm, and any other items that may help. Be careful, though. This is one way to get sucked into doing something beyond your riding ability.

Sometimes the best way to go faster is to actually slow down. By riding too aggressively, many riders work against themselves because they make too many mistakes. Remember, the more mistakes you make, the more tired you'll become.

Watch race coverage on television to see how professional racers tackle various race courses. Look at their race lines, passing techniques, and other strong points. Many athletes in professional sports such as baseball, football, and hockey study films extensively to learn more about themselves, their opponents, and the sport in general.

Practice braking later, but only do so in areas where you have plenty of runoff room in case you make a mistake. Braking later is one of the best ways to condition your senses to higher speeds.

Chapter 15

ADAPTING TO DIFFERENT BIKES
How Weight and Horsepower Affect Riding Technique

Whenever you switch from your usual bike to a different bike, you need to adjust your style to some degree. For example, let's say you and your buddy both ride 250s. You have a 1999 Honda CR, and your buddy rides a 2000 Yamaha YZ. When you switch, the bikes will feel markedly different, and you will have to adjust your riding style a bit to compensate. You might have to use the clutch a little bit more on the Honda to get the bike into the power, while the slightly better low-end of the Yamaha allows you to accelerate earlier without the clutch. These differences would be small enough that you would be able to ride with confidence, but significant enough to slow you down.

When switching between different bike sizes—say from a 125 to a 250—these differences become more dramatic. For some riders, adapting can be difficult. A classic example of someone who initially struggled to adapt is Ricky Carmichael. When he switched from 125s to 250s, he had to change his riding style. He was totally dominant on the 125, where his outside line, high cornering speed, and wide-open style left the rest of the field for dead. When he first started racing 250s, however, he was struggling a bit at first. His riding style wasn't as well-suited to the 250, and he had to make some changes in order to win. Of course, when you have Ricky Carmichael's talent, you are going to make this transition. The rest of us need this chapter.

Most riders enjoy 125s because they handle so well. The chassis is usually very similar to a 250, but most 125s usually weigh approximately 15 pounds less. This may not seem like a lot, but the decreased weight makes quite a difference. The bikes are easier to flick and the suspension works much better with the lower weight. The only weakness is that 125s have less horsepower than larger bikes and a narrow powerband. To go fast on a 125, you need to carry more speed than with larger bikes.

It's easy to see why the 250 is the most popular two-stroke engine displacement on the planet. In most cases it offers the best compromise between horsepower and weight. They have plenty of earth-churning, roost-throwing power, plus they are fairly nimble.

Because of their extraordinary power, open bikes are extremely potent and brutally fast. Precise throttle delivery and liberal clutch use are required to keep rear wheelspin to a minimum. The one disadvantage that most open bikes have is weight. Generally they are less maneuverable than 125s and 250s, which affects every aspect of riding, plus they have a tendency to tire riders easily.

Opposite: **Riding 80cc machines is typically very similar to riding a 125. The lack of engine displacement requires lots of engine rpm in order to build horsepower. Fast mini riders like Danny Carlson have to pay close attention to frequent gear changes along with constant clutch use and precise throttle control.**

Techniques for Different Size Bikes
80s and 125s

"There are huge differences in the various engine sizes and they all require different riding styles," says Mike Healey, who has raced virtually every size of two- and four-stroke motorcycles in National- and/or World Championship-caliber events. "When I rode 80s I remember that it was real important to keep the revs up, especially as I got bigger. Minis are pretty dead off bottom, but once they come alive, they can feel as fast as a 125."

"It's real important to pay attention to shifting on an 80," states Danny Carlson. "Most minis are pretty picky and won't work that well when ridden a gear too high or too low."

Most 80s are designed for teenagers because of the short seat height; hence, the engine is packaged in a small chassis. Typically, a 125 is the smallest displacement of a normal-size frame.

"On 125s you can be more aggressive in the turns than on a 250 mostly because of the weight," claims Mike Metzger. "You can hold the throttle on longer and accelerate much quicker because they handle better.

"Aboard 125s it's usually best to ride with your weight toward the back of the bike. This way you can keep the front end light and add traction to the rear wheel. Since 125s don't have as much power as the larger bikes, it's really important to maintain constant traction."

For riders moving up from 80s or those who want the best-handling full-size bike, 125s are a good choice. Although 125s can be difficult to ride due to the power delivery, they handle well, are easy to throw around,

and are a joy to ride. The 125s aren't as good for off-road and enduro riding, though, and aren't quite as flexible as the larger machines.

The 250s

Moving up in engine size, the 250s are the easiest to ride and have become the premier class in motocross racing. The powerband is broader, with more low-end than an 80 or 125. There is also enough power to accelerate out of mistakes. On a smaller bike, if you totally blow a corner, it will take some time (and clutch abuse) to get that lost momentum back. On a 250, momentum is only a twist of the wrist away. The final added benefit is that 250 engines tend to require less maintenance than a smaller bike. Considering all of this, it's no surprise that 250s are the best-selling two-strokes in the United States.

"Two-fifties offer the best of both worlds," Healey says. "They are much lighter than an open bike, yet they are way more powerful than a 125. I'd say a 250 is the best all-around size."

"I actually find that I have to concentrate more on 250s than on 125s," says Metzger. "Throttle control seems more important; otherwise, you can get in deep trouble pretty fast."

For most riders, 250s are the best choice. Power is ample and the powerband is broad and relatively easy to use. The motocross bikes usually have power that is flexible enough for a broad range of riding, and can be modified to work well in any kind of race. Enduro bikes like the Suzuki RMX250 and KTM 250E/XC can be ideal for more casual riders as well. They are a little easier to ride than motocross bikes, and work well for a broad range of conditions. You probably won't win a motocross race on one, but you could certainly race an occasional moto and have a good time. Whichever you choose, the only real drawback is that 250s tend to be more expensive, although since it is the most popular size, there are more machines available, at least in the used market.

Open Class Bikes

The larger open bikes (251cc and above) also require a totally different riding style. The power delivery used to be smoother than the smaller bikes, although modern open classers have a pretty awesome hit. Still, there is lots of low-end power on tap,

and open bikes don't require as much shifting. They also require less maintenance than smaller bikes.

"On open bikes, it's important to ride with your weight centered or slightly toward the front to keep it from wheelying," Healey says. "And because they're much heavier than the other bikes, you can't throw them around as much, plus you have to do your braking earlier to slow down in time."

"Most of the time it's better to ride an open bike a gear high. This will smooth out the low-end hit and will reduce the amount of shifting—they also won't vibrate as bad," claims Ron Lechien. "Truthfully, open bikes usually don't do that well when they're over-revved unless they have a lot of serious motor work done to them."

Open bikes are the bike of choice for desert racers, where their abundant power is needed to push the bikes through deep sand at high speeds. Big-bores can also work well for vet riders or trail riders. The advantages are an abundance of low-end power and lower maintenance costs. Keep in mind, however, that these bikes make a ton of horsepower and can get you into trouble very quickly. Without thoughtful throttle control, you'll end up on your head before you know it.

Thumpers

In the world of four-strokes, the horsepower-to-weight ratio is also important, but the effects are reduced for two reasons: In general four-strokes weigh more than comparably sized two-strokes, and secondly, they usually don't produce as much power. Therefore, engine displacement is typically larger to help compensate for the differences.

The most important difference with four-stroke engines is power delivery. They tend to give you a smooth, extremely broad powerband. Four-strokes don't rev as quickly as two-strokes, but the power is typically more controllable. In conditions where traction is hard to find, like slippery rocks or slimy off-camber turns, a four-stroke's more progressive power delivery will make it easier to handle, especially for lower-level riders. In deep sand or long straights, a four-stroke will give up some time to the two-stroke engines, which tend to have more top-end power and nearly instantaneous delivery. Honda XRs are classic examples, with controllable, easy-to-use power. You may not have as much as the guy next to you, but you'll be able to use all of it. Keep in mind, though, that this is changing a bit. Some of the high-end four-strokes are built for motocross, and have a powerband more like a two-stroke engine. Just the same, though, their advantage is hooking up out of the turns with a more progressive delivery of power.

"One of the coolest things about four-strokes is that they love to be flat-tracked around turns," says Healey, "especially big sweepers. Use this to your advantage if you're dicing with someone on a two-stroke."

"I usually ride a four-stroke like an open bike since the two handle real similar," says motocross and off-road champ Ty Davis. "I try to take wide lines whenever possible to conserve energy and to keep up momentum."

For off-road, trail, or beginning riders, a four-stroke is ideal. They are easier to ride, and typically require less maintenance than two-strokes. They are becoming more prevalent in the upper echelons of racing as well. Scott Summers has won several off-road championships on a Honda XR600, and Joel Smets (Husaberg) and Jacky Martens (Husqvarna) won the 500cc World Championship on four-strokes. As a final bonus, four-strokes can be made street legal in most states. While a converted off-road thumper wouldn't be the vehicle of choice to ride from New York to Los Angeles, they are great for getting from trail to trail or for short trips.

Choosing a Bike

If you are deciding which bike to buy, consider your riding level and places you will ride. A good way to get an idea of what suits you is to look at a wide assortment of bikes. If you look at used machines, you can often arrange to take a test ride. You might think that you want a motocross bike, but find in a test ride that the power delivery is too violent and a four-stroke or enduro bike is much better for you.

If motocross racing is your only desire, by all means look at a motocross bike. But keep in mind that motocross bikes are built for one purpose—racing on MX tracks—and they are a handful in most conditions, especially for riders who are just starting out. If you want to try a broad range of riding and are just getting started out, take a long hard look at other off-road bikes. Bikes like Kawasaki KDXs, Yamaha ITs, the Suzuki RMX, Honda XRs, and KTM E/XCs are a blast to ride and can handle almost any kind of terrain. As you read this book, you'll discover that a key to going fast is being relaxed and comfortable. That's hard to do when the bike delivers more power than you can use every time you open the throttle!

Chapter 16

STRATEGY
Power of the Mind

There's a lot more to racing than pinning the throttle and trying to ride your fastest. Any racer in any sport will tell you that there is always a strategy involved.

One of the most important aspects of strategy is simply having one. If you go to the gate with a plan, you'll be better prepared for the race. Obviously, a good strategy is better than a lousy one, but a plan is important for you to succeed.

Strategy can be applied on several levels, from passing strategy to a strategy for the season or for your career. It can apply to many different aspects of riding, from bike setup to setting up a pass. For starters, though, consider strategy that can be applied to a particular moto or race.

Race Log

A good place to start is with a race log or notebook. There is a useful sheet in chapter two that you can photocopy and use to record bike setup information. In addition to making notes about your bike, you should make notes about the track and your riding. Is there a section of the track where you were particularly fast? Did you crash? Where and why? Where did you get passed frequently? Also note any other significant things. Was it dusty? muddy? What was the traction like? Once you have ridden a track and written in your log book, you can review your notes the

Don't get caught up in mind games because they will wear you down, both on and off the track. Instead, concentrate on your own race program and how you can be a better rider.

night before or in the car on the way to race, and start to form your strategy.

If you don't have notes but have raced the course, take some time to remember what you can about the course. If possible, do a mental lap of the course, remembering as many details as you can. Figure out the sections in which you did well and those in which

you did poorly. Think about why you were fast or slow. What could you do differently to go faster? What do you need to continue doing to keep your advantage?

Walk the Track

The next important step is to walk the track. As you go around the track, match your

Winning races takes desire, determination, and hard work. Even when the chips are down, never give up. Steve Lamson faced a huge point deficit at the beginning of the 1995 season and ended up winning the AMA 125cc National Championship.

Always have some sort of strategy mapped out before you go to the starting line.

mental picture to what you see. Where have lines changed? Where can you pass? This is also a good time to talk to your race buddies and see what they are doing, especially if they are faster than you.

Also, consider how the track will change. If it's soft sand, you can expect ruts to form. If you know the track well, make a mental note of where ruts will form and how you can turn that to your advantage.

Visualize the Race

When you get back to the pits, take some time to sit down and imagine a lap. Focus on a simple thing to work on in each corner. If you are really into it, draw a map of the track and make a note at each obstacle.

In practice, try some of these strategies and adjust as necessary. This is an especially good time to try several different lines and get a feel for whether your theories

will work. Afterwards, go back to the pits and sit down again, adjusting your mental picture of the track.

Assembling Race Strategy

At this point, you have a picture of the track and how to attack it. Factor in the race conditions, number of competitors, quality of the competition, and your conditioning to form a strategy for the race.

For example, if it's a short race with lots of entrants and your conditioning is suspect, you'll want to concentrate on getting a good start, charging as hard as you can in the first lap, and conserving energy for the rest of the race. Let's say you conserve energy by slowing down a fraction in a long whoop section and into some wicked braking bumps since these two places sap a lot of energy. You could plan to be sure and use the best line to hold off any passes and concentrate on keep-

ing your speed up on the smoother parts of the track.

You'll probably want some kind of strategy for the start as well. Watch some starts, check out the best lines, and factor in your own personal style to come up with a sound strategy off the line.

When you come to the line, you should have several strategies in place: a plan of attack for the start, a general plan for the course of the race, and some specific ideas on fast lines and places to pass. This plan of attack will give you a better focus and is likely to get you better results, mainly because some of the questions that will come up during the race will already be answered.

Thinking Long-Term

Strategy also applies on a larger scale to riders competing in a series or making long-term goals with their riding. Your goal may be

STRATEGY

Remember, a key to success is strategy. Professionals got to where they are with hard work, talent, and a plan for success. Here is a sampling of some of the strategies used by the world's fastest riders:

Jeremy McGrath—"I always try to get to the front as fast as possible, then I try to open up a comfortable lead and, depending on how things are going, I know if I can let up or if I need to ride harder. Having a cushion is important because it means that you don't have to take as many chances in order to win."

Steve Lamson—"No matter what, it's important to never give up. In 1995, I was over 50 points down in the 125 National Championship and I didn't think winning was really possible. But I decided to give it my all and take each race one at a time. In the end, it came down to the final moto but I wound up winning. Had I given up at any time, the title would have gone to someone else."

Jeremy McGrath—"I always pay attention to my bike in practice and in each moto so I can make any necessary changes for my next ride."

Ron Lechien—"Part of the strategy is to find places to pass in practice and then remember them later. I always try every line in practice so I know what works and what doesn't."

Mike Kiedrowski—"I walk part of the track before each moto so I can see how the lines have changed. This helps out a lot, especially the first lap of the race."

Danny Carlson—"The night before the race, I try to get really good sleep. I go to bed at the normal time and then get up early enough to take a shower, and eat breakfast on the way to the track."

Steve Lamson—"After practice and between motos I try to get as much rest as possible."

Danny Carlson—"I always go to the bathroom before I go to the line. During a race you can't stop and I find that I don't ride that well when I'm uncomfortable."

Mike Kiedrowski—"I usually have someone videotape practice so I can see what I and the other riders are doing right and wrong. This really helps out a lot."

Scott Summers—"At races where I know there will be a pit stop, I try to have everything organized so I can get in and get out. I have a plan ahead of time that includes refueling, getting new goggles, and gloves, if I need them, plus replacing any broken parts. I always have all of my tools laid out in plain view, where they are easy to grab, and I have spare bars and wheels ready to go."

Steve Hatch—"I always want to know as much about the course as I can, so I always try to walk it. I look for anything that can give me an advantage to help me win."

Ty Davis—"At enduros, I always pay close attention to my mileage and time. When I come in early, I try to check my bike over to make sure there are no problems."

Scott Summers—"It's a good idea to make sure that your mechanic is really familiar with your bike and understands everything about the type of racing that you're doing. My mechanic, Fred Bramblett, is one of the best because he thinks like a racer and knows that some races are decided in the pits. There's nothing worse than coming in for fuel and having your pit crew running over each other as they try to take care of things."

Larry Roeseler—"In extremely long races like Baja or Six-Days, you have to make sure your equipment lasts, otherwise you may not be able to finish."

Scot Harden—"In dusty races you never want to follow people for too long because it can be dangerous and because it will ruin your air filter. Dust will only slow you down, that's why I will always do whatever is possible to get around a rider who's dusting me out."

a national championship or simply to bring your riding up and compete in your first race. Whatever it is, take a little time to make a plan that will guide you toward your goal. In any type of series race, the idea is usually to score as many points as possible at each round, even if it means riding with failing equipment, hence the phrase "every point counts." For the rider planning a first race, some conditioning, a regular riding schedule, and showing up for a practice day or two at the track could be a good strategy.

STRATEGY

- You can't win if you don't finish.
- Never give up.
- If you are racing a championship, think long term.
- Avoid riding injured.
- Pay attention to bike setup during practice.
- Walk as much of the course as possible before your race.
- Avoid following other riders.
- Don't take any unnecessary chances.
- In off-road races that require pits, make sure they are organized, speedy, and efficient.

"Part of any strategy requires finishing," said Bob Hannah. "You have to be mentally strong in any race, and that means knowing that your bike can do its job."

Part of any off-road strategy should include pit stops. Always have all of your tools and spare parts organized and easily accessible in order to speed up work time.

Think to win. Conditioning, practice, and training are all important to finding the front of the pack, but your brain is your most powerful weapon on the track.

RELATED SECTIONS:ALL

#46 LOOK AHEAD

Look far enough ahead of you to be ready for what's coming up. If you can't see it (because of an obstacle), remember what's there.

This is one of those things that most riders don't even think about, but it's very important and it's not really a natural thing for most riders. It has to be learned and practiced. The most common mistake is not looking ahead far enough and soon enough. Don't race the track by every 10 feet. Race it one section at a time and blend the sections together with a purpose. When done correctly, it's an art form. When you go beyond that, it's magic.

You should always be scanning the track in front of you, focusing on the most important things, then scanning and focusing on the next most important thing, and so on. If you can't see it, keep remembering what's there. You should ride with this main focus and your peripheral vision. Always be ready for what's coming up well before you get there. Set yourself up so you're going to be on the right line well in advance. And if you're trying to pass someone, look beyond them, not at them.

You can't win races by following people.

"Whether you think you can or think you can't, you are right."

—Henry Ford

Forming a plan is half the battle to success on the track. Here Brian Swink gets a word or two of advice.

Chapter 17

FOUR-STROKES
How To Use This Different Type of Motor to Your Advantage

Since the introduction of the YZ400F, four-strokes have transformed from off-road-only machines to capable threats on any race course (i.e., motocross track) in the country. When Doug Henry won the 1998 AMA 250cc National Motocross Championship on the YZ400F, notice was officially given that thumpers were back with a vengeance. The addition of aggressive thumpers from Yamaha, Canondale, Husaberg, Suzuki, Honda, and KTM have made a four-stroke a legitimate consideration for any off-road rider.

While engine design is the biggest distinguishing factor between a four-stroke and its reed-valve relative, the type of power delivery affects every aspect of performance. Braking, suspension, and even starting procedures are influenced by the four-stroke power plant, thus mandating a different type of riding style. Sure, there are a lot of shared traits, but if you know the differences between the two types of engines, you will be a better rider.

Deep ruts are a four-stroke rider's enemy. Berms, on the other hand, are a four-stroke rider's savior. Take the outside line, get on the throttle early, and use the berm to take advantage of the thumper's power and speed.

Motor

Depending on the type of bike and whether or not it has an automatic- or manual-compression release, something as simple as starting a four-stroke can be a challenge. Typically, four-strokes are more difficult to start than two-strokes, but once you get the procedure figured out, it shouldn't be intimidating.

From the first moment you let the clutch out, you will notice that the four-stroke's power delivery is different than the two-stroke's. In general, four-strokes produce less wheelspin and more traction. This is a definite advantage during acceleration, but how a four-stroke builds momentum is what makes it so unique.

In most cases, four-strokes don't respond well to excessive clutch use. While the clutch can be effective in many instances, it's not nearly as important as it is on two-strokes. Generally, four-strokes work best when the throttle is applied in a roll-on fashion. These motors produce a lot of torque down low, and the addition of the extra parts, such as a cam

A broad powerband and torquey delivery can pay off big on the starting line. Similar to a two-stroke, the key is smoothly letting out the clutch and steadily—quickly!—rolling on the throttle. Do some practice starts near the line if you can to determine how hard you can drop the clutch and hammer the throttle without excessive wheelspin. With some practice and a thumper, your odds of getting the holeshot will improve.

STARTING A FOUR-STROKE

Scott Summers—"Avoid half-kicks that many riders use to start two-strokes. Larger four-strokes will only start if you kick them all the way through."

Doug Dubach—"Use the compression release to get the piston just past top dead center to start. The compression release is there for a reason."

Larry Roeseler—"Most four-strokes don't require any throttle to get them started. Be careful not to 'crack' the throttle like you would on two-strokes. If you're worried that you will do it out of habit, then take your hand off the throttle and place it somewhere else on the handlebar—like on top of your master cylinder."

Randy Hawkins—"If you have a hot start button, always use it to start a warm bike. It will make carburetion corrections automatically, and will save you a lot of hassle."

While two-stroke bikes favor cut-and-thrust riding, four-strokes are better at wide lines. The explosiveness of a two-stroke engine allows the rider to come close to a stop in a corner (as when you square off a corner inside a berm) and accelerate hard enough to maintain or gain time on the rider in the outside line. Four-stroke riders don't have that luxury. Smooth power and a heavier bike mean cut and thrust is not the technique of choice. Go wide, roll on the throttle early, and tractor out of the corners. This technique worked well for Doug Henry, who won a Supercross and a National Outdoor title on the YZ400F.

chain and cam(s), increases spinning mass, which means that "double clutching it" doesn't build engine rpm as quickly to provide added boost. Hence, consistent throttle application with minimal clutch use is usually more effective.

You should also note that four-strokes are usually a little bit more sluggish during the beginning of acceleration, because the motor makes most of its power in midrange and on top. This means that if a four-stroke were to drag race a two-stroke, the two-stroke may get

the initial jump from a dead stop (if the two bikes are similar in performance), but the four-stroke will receive a power surge in midrange, and should be able to make up ground and beat the other machine to the next obstacle. This is, of course, in general

Four-strokes tend to wheelie out of traction-filled corners more than any other bike. That's why good four-stroke riders have their weight centered or on the front of the bike most of the time, whereas two-stroke riders tend to hang off the back.

terms, but four-stroke boost is most appreciated toward the end of a straightaway rather than the beginning. This is why four-strokes have traditionally proved to be the most effective motor design when riding in mud and over off-camber terrain, where too much wheelspin can actually be detrimental.

If the clutch is used too much on a four-stroke, it generally can't withstand the abuse. In most cases it will overheat and fade rather quickly. Once this happens, it probably won't come back during a race and it will increase your chances of stalling the engine.

On tight tracks it's usually more effective to seek out wider lines that allow momentum to be carried. This way you can stay in the meat of the power charge more effectively to the next obstacle. Of course, this depends on the size of the engine and the sheer number of performance modifications. A rule of thumb is that the larger the motor, the more line choices are offered. For example, even though Doug Henry and Jimmy Button ride works Yamaha YZ400s, they have to take wider lines in Supercross than their 250 two-stroke counterparts. They need a better run at

While fanning the clutch is a key technique on a two-stroke (particularly small-bore bikes), it is not as important on a four-stroke. A four-stroke's smooth power delivery allows you to get on the gas earlier in the corner and roll into the powerband rather than clutch into it, as with a two-stroke. On occasion, of course, even four-stroke riders use the clutch to get to the meat of the powerband. Too much use can cost you the race, however. Once a four-stroke clutch is roasted, you won't get it back until the engine has had plenty of time to cool off.

Because of their increased weight—usually 10 to 20 pounds more than a two-stroke—thumpers are harder to throw around. Obviously, this can be a disadvantage, but new technology is making four-strokes much lighter and more flickable.

whoops, have to be more precise on technical obstacles, and generally find it less beneficial to square-off corners.

In contrast, on high-speed outdoor courses, bikes like the YZ400 can be ridden in the area of the powerband where power can be used more effectively. This means they can seek out more inside lines and aren't as restricted.

One of the major advantages that four-strokes offer is their ability to corner fast without berms or ruts. Because they accelerate smoothly and usually don't produce a whole lot of wheelspin, they can be ridden quite effectively on flat turns. Simply roll on the throttle, shift your body weight forward, and hang on for an amazing ride. On high-speed courses, this provides four-stroke riders with more options to shave lap times and make passes.

The biggest disadvantage is when four-strokes are required to come to a dead stop. It's difficult for riders not to become overaggressive and slip the clutch. Some slippage

can be effective, but it must be done in moderation and very briefly. Off-road riders who ride in wooded areas will also experience this problem, but will have a number of ways to deal with the situation. When possible, avoid coming to a dead stop. Try to maintain enough momentum so you don't run the risk of stalling and have instant power on tap.

Tight, technical riding is where motor performance really comes into play. High-compression engines, usually associated with a lot of high-performance modifications, can be a double-edged sword. In some cases they can be great for fast acceleration and in minimizing clutch abuse. But on the other hand, they can sometimes increase the opportunity for stalling and therefore mandate more clutch use: It all depends on the situation.

High-compression engines have another significant characteristic. Since they offer more engine braking, you must watch out when jumping. Four-strokes have a tendency to jump front-wheel low if the throttle is

chopped too early. This aspect takes a little time for familiarization, and it's certainly something you must keep in mind at all times.

Braking

Unlike with two-strokes, the use of the front and rear brakes isn't as important on a thumper. Most four-strokes have enough compression during deceleration that they actually slow down quite effectively—kind of like a Jake Brake on a semi truck. This type of braking can be highly effective, but it all depends on engine displacement and motor modifications. Typically, the larger the motor and higher the compression, the faster the engine will slow down a bike.

To use this technique, you must allow the bike to stay in gear while decelerating and make sure the clutch is not disengaged. Using this technique actually gives you more control over the motorcycle because the dynamic forces of engaging and disengaging the clutch can actually upset suspension

Short-approach, high-speed jumps are particularly tricky with four-strokes. Because of four-strokes' quick acceleration, it can sometimes be tricky to determine correct body position on takeoffs for short-approach, high-speed jumps. They can even fool talented riders like former multi-time National Champion Doug Henry.

and negatively influence traction. When this happens, it usually makes riders back off the throttle too much to make corrections on body positioning. Usually when you use engine braking, you don't have to readjust body positioning as much.

This technique is most effective on flat surfaces because there is a higher likelihood that you can stall the engine in areas such as whoops or ruts. In most cases, engine braking will cause the rear wheel to slide out slightly while the tire searches desperately for traction. A classic example of this is in dirt track racing, where riders use engine braking to let the rear wheel step out in a technique they call "backing it into a corner." On extremely smooth surfaces, this is where four-strokes are much more effective than two-strokes.

Cornering

Because of the type of power delivery and its dislike for clutch abuse, most four-strokes tend to search for wider lines. Though in some instances an inside line can

Four-strokes tend to come off jumps front-wheel low due to engine compression (it's like dragging your rear brake on the takeoff of a jump). This effect has been lessened on the YZ400F and other MX-oriented four-strokes, but it is still present. As a rider, you need to either compensate with light throttle during takeoffs or use it to your advantage. In this photo, Doug Henry uses engine braking to set up for a rare inside line after this short, but steep, tabletop.

be more effective, the rule of thumb is to go wide. This actually gives you a lot more freedom over two-strokes, or at least, gives you different options.

The biggest advantages come on flat ground or off-cambers. This is due to the smooth power delivery provided by the four-stroke engine and the lack of wheelspin produced. This is especially true in slippery conditions such as mud or hardpack surfaces.

Four-strokes really don't like to square corners and rarely is this technique effective. They also don't like being double-clutched, or have the clutch slipped for extended periods of time. What they do like is the throttle rolled on with the rider's weight centered over the gas tank and handlebar. They are also very effective in shallow ruts, but usually don't like deep ruts because these can overheat the clutch if the rider isn't careful.

Jumping

Because of engine braking, jumping a thumper can be extremely different than jumping a two-stroke. For starters, many two-stroke riders "chop" the throttle on the face of a jump instead of powering all the way off the takeoff ramp. If you were to do this on a four-stroke, you would most likely find that the bike would slow dramatically and cause the front end to drop immediately after liftoff. This also has the tendency to cause riders to jump way short. This can be especially dangerous on short "kicker" jumps.

Still, many riders do like to chop the throttle, and this can be O.K. and safe as long as you make body positioning adjustments to accommodate rapid slowing. Typically, this means shifting weight to the back of the bike to keep the front wheel from dropping as the bike becomes airborne.

Suspension

Typically, four-stroke suspension is more plush than two-stroke suspension. It generally responds better to small and mid-size bumps, but usually doesn't offer the same resistance to bottoming. This is good news for techniques like engine braking because it will keep the wheels in contact with the ground more effectively, and it can also be good for whoops. Generally, four-strokes are more effective in whoops because of smooth power delivery and typically better rear suspension action.

Unfortunately, because four-strokes are heavier than two-strokes, they also bottom out much more easily. This means the suspension collapses more on takeoffs and G-outs, and on big jumps and/or poorly timed landings.

FOUR-STROKES

- **Let the motor help you slow down. Four-strokes offer excellent engine braking.**
- **Don't abuse the clutch. Four-strokes overheat easily and most clutches will fade when used like a two-stroke.**
- **Pay attention when chopping the throttle on jump faces. Engine braking may lower the engine too fast and can cause the front end to drop suddenly on takeoff.**
- **Four-strokes crave flat turns, so don't always seek out ruts and berms as your first two options.**
- **Power delivery of four-stroke engines provides lots of traction and can be an advantage in mud, off-camber corners, and at motocross-style starts. Remembering this will give you more confidence when racing or riding against two-strokes.**

Once you get the bike straight and tracking, the plush suspension and broad power make four-strokes excel at skimming whoops. Setting up for the section requires a longer approach to build speed effectively. Note that Doug Henry is in perfect position, letting the bike soak up the hits and skimming through the whoops on his YZ-F.

Appendix

Magazines, Web Sites, Books, Instructional Videos, and Riding Schools

The intention of Pro Motocross and Off-Road Riding Techniques is to make you a more informed rider and discuss some of the theories involved in off-road riding. To further enhance your riding skills, you may want to check out some of the motorcycle riding schools, instructional videos, and off-road magazines that are on the market.

Motorcycle Magazines

Magazines are a great source for tuning tips, as well as new bike tests and product reviews. More important, they are a good way to keep in touch with your sport. Some of the following magazines can be found at your dealer or at the newsstand. If not, contact the publisher to subscribe.

American Motorcyclist
P.O. Box 6114
Westerville, OH 43081
614/891-2425

The publication of the American Motorcyclist Association (AMA). Street and dirt coverage; great listing of dates, times, and contacts for amateur races and events. Monthly.

Cycle News
2201 Cherry Avenue
Long Beach, CA 90806
310/427-7433
subscribe@cyclenews.com
www.cyclenews.com

U.S. and international motorcycle racing (all forms). Race reports, profiles, inside info. Great classifieds. The publication for timely race results. Weekly.

Cycle World
853 W. 17th Street
Costa Mesa, CA 92627
714/720-5300

General interest magazine for motorcycle enthusiasts (street-oriented). Includes occasional off-road or motocross bike shootout or test. Occasional off-road product review. Monthly.

Dirt Bike
25233 Anza Drive
Valencia, CA 91355
805/295-1910

Covers motocross and off-road riding. New bike tests, product tests, riding tips, maintenance tips, and race reports. Monthly.

Dirt Rider
6420 Wilshire Blvd.
Los Angeles, CA 90048-5515
800/800-3478

Covers motocross and off-road riding. New bike tests, product tests, riding tips, maintenance tips, race reports. Lists two riding areas each month. Monthly.

Motocross Action
25233 Anza Drive
Valencia, CA 91355
805/295-1910

Covers motocross riding. New bike tests, product tests, maintenance tips, race reports. Monthly.

Motocross Journal
25233 Anza Drive
Valencia, CA 91355
805/295-1910

Motocross only. Rider, tuner, and team owner profiles. Race reports, more. Includes regular vintage motocross bike feature and profiles of past motocross racing heroes. Six issues per year.

Motorcyclist
6420 Wilshire Boulevard
Los Angeles, CA 90048-5515
303/678-0354

General interest magazine for motorcycle enthusiasts (street bikes only). Monthly.

Old Bike Journal
1010 Summer Street
Stamford, CT 06905
203/425-8777

Focuses on old and classic bikes. Includes occasional features on vintage motocross bikes and racing. Good classifieds for vintage bikes. Six issues per year.

Racer X
Route 7, Box 459
Morgantown, WV 26505
304/594-1157

Racy, alternative look at motocross lifestyle. Monthly.

Sport Rider
6420 Wilshire Boulevard
Los Angeles, CA 90048-5515
303/678-0354

Street bikes only. Hard-core sport riding and racing. Monthly.

Tex-Mx News
200 Madeline Ln.
Burleson, TX 76028
817/295-6397

Regional motocross race reports serving Texas and Oklahoma. Monthly.

Trail Rider Magazine
P.O. Box 129
Medford, NJ 08055
609/953-7805

Eastern off-road riding and racing. Dual sports. Bike tests. Monthly.

Internet Sites

The Internet has been steadily improving as a source for dirt bike stuff. Race reports, classifieds, manufacturers, suppliers, and shops can all be found on the Internet. Also, once you find a few sites, you can check the related links section and find hundreds more. At the time this book was published, some of the biggest and best are listed below. By the time you see this, there will be hundreds more.

Motorcycle Online
http://motorcycle.com/motorcycle.html

General-interest motorcycle site. Features, race reports (available by e-mail and online), product reviews, classifieds, and much more.

Cycle News Site
www.cyclenews.com/

Motorcycle news. Race reports (condensed), short features, more. Also a great site.

Whip It!
www.visualradio.com/whipit/

Dirt-related site

The Official Jeremy McGrath Site

www.nacnac.com

Four-time Supercross Champion Jeremy McGrath has his own home page. Decent photos posted, a few comments from Jeremy, and a Gary Semics riding technique.

Motorcycle Books

There are a number of books available on motocross and off-road racing. The list below gives some of the better examples. Look for them at your local bookstore, motorcycle dealership or parts store, or call 1-800-826-6600 for a free catalog from Motorbooks International, which stocks all of these books.

Motocross and Off-Road Motorcycle Performance Handbook

By Eric Gorr

MBI Publishing Company, 1996

Turn your motocross or off-road bike into a racing weapon. You'll find everything you need to know and more, from building the ultimate high-rpm outdoor screamer to the inside tips that the manual doesn't tell you. Includes specific tuning tips for most off-road bikes, as well as suspension tuning, engine tuning, and rebuilding of every system on the bike.

Freestyle Motocross

By Garth Milan

MBI Publishing Company, 2000

The first book to cover the exciting, new sport of freestyle motocross. Pro riders Mike Metzger, Kris Rourke, Ronnie Faisst, Larry Linkogle, and Brian Deegan explain in step-by-step sequences how they pull off tricks such as the Bar Hop, Heel Clicker, Cordova, Superman Seat Grab, Cliffhanger, and others.

Monkey Butt!

By Rick Sieman

Rick Sieman Racing, 1995

A collection of essays from former Dirt Bike magazine editor Rick "Super Hunky" Sieman. Sieman's writing is highly entertaining, and his more serious bits offer an eye-opening look at the motorcycle industry.

Gary Bailey Teaches Rider Technique

By Gary Bailey

Gary Bailey, 1986

Gary Bailey has long been known as the professor of off-road racing technique. In this book, he offers his techniques and tactics, as demonstrated by his son, ex-champion David Bailey. This book is a bit long in the tooth, but most of the riding techniques still apply.

A Twist of the Wrist

By Keith Code

Acrobat Books

This classic on road racing techniques has a lot of strategy and mental preparation tips that can be adapted to off-road racing. Don't expect to learn how to clear a triple, but the concepts of $10 worth of attention, focusing on parts of the track you need work on, and developing a strategy to keep racing from driving you to bankruptcy are all applicable.

Major Race Promoters And Sanctioning Bodies

American Motorcyclist Association

P.O. Box 6114

Westerville, OH 43081

614/891-2425

National Motosport Association

P.O. Box 46

Norwalk, CA 90650

310/868-8112

Racer Productions

Route 7, Box 459

Morgantown, WV 26505

304/594-1157

Riding Schools and Instruction Video Distributors

Gary Bailey Video/MX Schools

P.O. Box 130

Axton, VA 24054

703/650-1759

Tony D Motocross Schools

345 John Hyde Rd.

New Windsor, MD 21776

410/635-6916

Donnie Hansen Motocross Academy

1174 Whitney Dr.

Yuba City, CA 95991

916/755-2799

Mike Healey MX School

3209 Colorado Pl.

Costa Mesa, CA 92626

714/435-1741

Rocket Rex Racing

10001 Choiceana Ave.

Hesperia, CA 92345

619/949-4193

Marty Smith Motocross Clinic

2486 Eltinge Dr.

Alpine, CA 91901

619/659-0273

Gary Semics Motocross Schools

1000 Southridge Drive

Salem, OH 44460

330/337-3020

If you've been wanting to go to a motocross school but there hasn't been one in your area at the right time, the Gary Semics Motocross School has a solution. Gary is training and certifying instructors to teach under his school's name and format. As of June 2000 there are four active instructors.

In the southeastern United States:

Ike De Jager

107 Quartermain Court

Carry, NC 27513

919/461-0558

mx411@bellsouth.net

In Texas and the western United States:

Larry Morton

23047 Benbury Drive

Katy, TX 77450

281/693-6488

GSMXSco@gateway.net

In the central United States:

Shannon Niday

15245 Metcalf Avenue

Shawnee Mission, KS 66223

913/908-7494

pharteam@aol.com

In Argentina, South America:

Jorge Martin

John O'Connor 122

8400 San Carlos De Bariloche

Rio Negro, Argentina, South America

0944-32930

jmarti@bariloche.com.ar

Gary's future plans are to have the entire United States covered. For more information, call the headquarters at 330/337-3020.

Glossary

Aftermarket Parts: Parts produced by a company other than the original equipment manufacturer.

Bore: A term used to describe one dimension of an engine's cylinder.

CC: Abbreviation for cubic centimeter.

Cross-rutted: A term used for describing what happens when one wheel accidentally comes out of a rut.

Double: Two jumps in succession that are jumped in one single leap.

Endo: A description of a bike uncontrollably flipping over frontward.

Ergonomics: A term used to describe the relationship between man and machine.

Four-stroke: A piston engine that fires on every fourth stroke. Intake and exhaust are controlled with mechanically actuated valves. Power output from these engines is typically smoother and more controllable than with two-stroke engines, but the valvetrain makes the engines a bit heavier. The other type of engine used in dirt bikes is a two-stroke, which fires every other stroke. Most motocross and off-road bikes use two-stroke engines, although that may be changing.

Gyroscopic: A physics term used to describe an object spinning on an axis. The gyroscopic effect is essential in many aspects for maintaining balance on a motorcycle.

Hardpack: Extremely hard terrain that provides little traction.

Headshake: A description of motorcycle handling when the handlebars shake uncontrollably from side to side.

High-side: Describes the action that occurs when a rider falls over on the outside while leaning into a turn or swapping out of control.

Hot line: Slang for the best line choice.

Knobbies: The small portion of tire tread that creates traction. Knobbies come in a wide range of patterns for all types of off-road riding.

Loop-out: When the front wheel comes so high off the ground that the bike actually flips over backwards.

Low-side: Describes the action that occurs when a rider falls over on the inside while leaning into a turn.

Master link: The connecting point of the chain.

MX: Abbreviation for motocross.

Nose-dive: A description of the attitude of a bike when the front wheel is substantially lower than the rear wheel.

Open bike: Typically a machine with a displacement larger than 251cc.

Outcropping: A clump of earth, usually rock in nature, that sticks off the side of a mountain.

Overrev: The act of allowing an engine to exceed its effective rpm range.

Powerband: A term used to describe the useful power of an engine. Moreover, the powerband stretches from bottom-end (low rpm), midrange, and top-end (high rpm).

Preload: A term used to describe how much force is applied to a spring at rest. Moreover, preload is generally used to describe fork and shock springs.

Pre-run: A term used in off-road racing that describes practice. Pre-running is essentially riding the course before the race in order to get an idea of the terrain, layout, speeds, etc.

R&D: Abbreviation for research and development.

Sag: A term used for describing how much suspension drops when a bike is not being ridden and is off the stand. Sag is usually measured in millimeters and it plays an important role in motorcycle setup.

Shim: A thin piece of metal used to take up space.

Sidewalls: The sides of the tire where there are knobs.

Square off: A term used for turning extremely sharply with the rear wheel locked up.

Swap: A description of the uncontrollable action when the rear wheel of a motorcycle bounces from side to side.

Swingarm: The large metallic object that connects the rear wheel to the frame and the shock.

Tabletop: A jump similar to a double since it has both takeoff and landing ramps, but the middle section is filled in with dirt.

Tacky: A description of soil that provides traction that's so good that it's almost sticky.

Trials: A type of motorcycle riding and competition that requires precise balance to negotiate a wide range of jagged, slippery, and odd-shaped obstacles at extremely slow speeds. Participants are penalized for dabbing a foot and are timed in order to decide a tie. Each rider rides the course solo and points are tallied up after riders have completed a series of courses.

Triple: Three jumps in succession that are jumped in one single leap.

Triple clamp: The portion of the motorcycle that connects the handlebar to the frame and the fork.

Two-stroke: A piston engine that fires on every other stroke. Intake and exhaust are controlled with ports in the cylinder. Modern engines typically use reed valves in the intake tract and mechanically operated exhaust valves, which change the size of the exhaust port. The only other type of engine used in common dirt bikes is a four-stroke, which uses valves to control intake and exhaust. Two-stroke engines are more common in dirt bikes, but that is slowly changing.

Wheelbase: The distance between the front and back wheel.

Index